A MIR

YOUR POCKET

Rosemary Ellen Guiley, Ph.D.

Thorsons

Thorsons
An Imprint of HarperCollins*Publishers*
77–85 Fulham Palace Road
Hammersmith, London W6 8JB

The Thorsons website address is www.thorsons.com

Thorsons is trademark of
HarperCollins*Publishers*

First published by Thorsons 2001

1 3 5 7 9 10 8 6 4 2

Rosemary Ellen Guiley asserts the moral right to
be identified as the author of this work

A catalogue record for this book is available
from the British Library

ISBN 0–00–711530–X

Printed and bound in Great Britain by
Martins the Printers, Berwick upon Tweed

ACKNOWLEDGEMENTS

I would like to express my deep appreciation to those who shared their personal stories of miracles for this book: Yvette Bigger, Robert H. Coxon, Carol Warner, Dolores Warner, Margarita Gurri and Jess Gurri, Elaine, Guy R., Juli, Louis P. and Rachel. I would also like to thank Dr Joan Pizzino and Carol R. Resch for permission to quote from their accounts: *The Story of My Miracle* by Dr Joan Pizzino and *The Feather* by Carol R. Resch.

A very special thank you goes to Mary Ellen, known as the 'Angel Scribe', for her support of this book. Mary Ellen is the author of *Expect Miracles* and *A Christmas Filled With Miracles* and is creator and editor of the free *Angels and Miracles* Good-News-Letter, at www.AngelScribe.com.

More about Robert Coxon and his incredible, inspiring music can be found at www.robertcoxon.com and www.kryon.com. And for Margarita Gurri's work with children, family relations and domestic violence, go to www.grace-works4kids.com.

Out of respect for privacy and personal sensitivities, I have followed the wishes of some of those interviewed by not using their full names and other details.

CONTENTS

INTRODUCTION

Miracles are a mystery that fascinates us. Miracles are events for which we can find no good or rational explanation, which seem to involve divine intervention – and which often leave us profoundly changed. Miracles have been documented through history, and are important to our religious, social, scientific and metaphysical views. They form part of our truth of life.

The traditional view that miracles happen *to* us – that we are passive recipients of a divine favour – is under increasing challenge. Science and metaphysics are finding they have great common ground in explaining the workings of the universe. Discoveries in science about the underlying interconnected nature of all things, combined with experiential knowledge about our powers of consciousness, are revealing a more intriguing picture of miracles. The picture shows that we help to create miracles as much as receive them. The miracle flows from a partnership, an elegant dance, of the divine and human.

We have an activist role, whether we know it or not. Our role in bringing miracles into manifestation requires responsible thought and action on our part.

Reality is the product of dynamic co-creation by God's will and human will. When human will is elevated to divine will and the two are in a concert of oneness, harmony is established and incredible manifestation is possible.

Rather than stand in awe of miracles, we need to understand them, and to understand the powers within us that are part of their creation. This book explores the many facets of miracles and their manifestation, as well as ways we can activate the miracle-creating ability within us.

Rosemary Ellen Guiley, Ph.D.

CHAPTER ONE

WHEN THE ORDINARY BECOMES THE EXTRAORDINARY

 By the time she was 16, Tina had been raped, sexually abused and physically beaten for five years.

She had denied that the abuse was going on, but at age 16 she could no longer hold the terrible secret. Her abuser was arrested and tried in court, but Tina's testimony was discredited and he was acquitted. Tina's life disintegrated. She fell prey to drugs and more abuse, and ran away from home.

When it seemed life couldn't get any worse, Tina reached a turning point. She made a courageous decision to confront her past and heal it. But she had barely begun therapy when she was given devastating news: she had ovarian cancer. There were three spots on one ovary, so distinct and developed that they could be seen with the naked eye. Her prognosis was grim. What she needed to stay alive was a miracle.

A miracle didn't seem likely, however. For Tina, it was the final blow to a scarred and unhappy life. 'I might as well die,' she told her therapist, Carol Warner. The injustice of it all was bitter.

The news of the cancer was equally devastating for Carol, who had known Tina and other members of her family for many years. Now she felt helpless in the face of the disease.

At home that night, Carol prayed for Tina and for guidance concerning how to help her. She did not pray specifically for healing, but for help in accordance with God's will. As she prayed, she felt her heart go out to Tina in a deep and profound way. She so sincerely wanted to help her.

In the middle of the night, something mysterious happened. Carol dreamed a dream that seemed so vivid as to be real. In the dream, the Blessed Virgin Mary floated down from above, surrounded by, and dressed in, the most beautiful blue colour. The energy around her was amazing and awe-inspiring. Carol became aware that Tina also was present in the dream, but was invisible. Instead of seeing Tina, Carol somehow viewed what she knew were the girl's ovaries.

As Mary came closer to Carol, she sent out three luminous globes of light. Carol knew that each one of the globes was going to one of the spots on Tina's diseased ovary. She saw each spot surrounded completely by a beautiful, glowing globe.

Carol emerged into waking. She knew with the most profound and inexplicable certainty that she had just witnessed Tina's complete healing. The cancer was gone.

Despite her conviction, Carol debated whether to share the dream with Tina. Carol was experienced in working with dreams, which usually have symbolic rather than literal meanings. She wondered if she were interpreting the dream correctly. She also questioned whether sharing the dream might raise false hopes in Tina. She finally decided to tell her.

With hope renewed, Tina went back to her doctor, who was astonished to find no trace of the cancerous lesions. A biopsy showed Tina to be cancer-free. Tina could barely contain her joy. She had no doubt that

Mother Mary had indeed healed her. Tina had got her miracle!

Relieved and overjoyed herself, Carol nonetheless continued to ponder just what had taken place that night. She believed in miracles and the power of prayer, and felt that she had been privileged to witness a miraculous healing.

How can this miracle be explained? Why did the healing involve a dream and Mother Mary? Carol was not Catholic and had prayed only for divine help in accordance with the highest good. The prayer had not been addressed to Mary. Tina was Catholic, though not particularly devout. Carol had been active for years in dreamwork, both professionally and personally, and knew dreams to be potent with meaning and power.

Healing within dreams has been documented since ancient times. For example, records from the sacred dream temples of Greek and Roman times report that all kinds of ailments and conditions were cured with the help of dreams, from chronic illnesses to blindness and lameness. People made pilgrimages to the temples to undergo ritual dreaming, in which they hoped the gods of healing would visit them and heal them.

Healing in dreams is reported in modern times, too. Typically, a person has an unusual and vivid dream in which they see or experience themselves being healed. The healing is later verified physically, and no 'rational' medical explanation can be made.

In this case, however, the dream occurred not to Tina but to her psychotherapist. Would the healing have happened without the dream?

Complex dynamics are involved in why and how a miracle happens. We will examine those dynamics in more detail later in this book, but now let's turn to some other ways miracles have changed lives.

ANGELIC RESCUE

When Jess Gurri was about five-and-a-half years old, the neighbours across the street had brand new kittens, and she wanted to see them. One afternoon as dusk was setting in, her pregnant mother, Margarita Gurri, took her by the hand and led her across the street. Jess skipped along. They were about halfway across when a car suddenly appeared, driving very fast and on the wrong side of the road. Margarita made an instinctive prayer to Mother Mary and tried to push Jess to hurry ahead of her, but the little girl froze in panic and then started to move backwards. The car began to swerve over the road and headed straight for the child. Suddenly Jess seemed to be flying through the air, as though she'd taken a mighty jump from a standing position, or someone had given her a giant push. She landed on the pavement on the opposite side of the road, teetered, and then righted herself. The car roared past them without slowing down.

As Margarita raced to her daughter and embraced her, she caught a glimpse of a shimmering, winged shape taking leave. 'Did you see that?' she cried. 'Yes,' Jess answered almost matter-of-factly. 'It's my guardian angel.'

Jess had felt the pressure of hands on her back and at first thought her mother pushed her. But Margarita had not, and there was no way that a human push could have sent her to safety – certainly without sprawling on the ground and getting injured. Jess's back was red where she had felt the pressure – the mark of a messenger of God. It was a miracle.

A GIFT FROM THE OTHER SIDE

Juli experienced a different kind of miracle than physical healing or rescue. It was an unusual miracle, in which something tangible was brought from another realm and left behind in the physical world.

Juli grew up in an Irish Catholic family in Chicago. Her mother, Colleen, was a woman of strong character but literally weak in the heart, due to rheumatic fever in childhood. Childbearing was dangerous for her, but she was determined to have a family, and have one she did. Juli was the third of four children. She and her mother were very close. Once they made a pact that whoever died first would do everything in her power to give the other one some sort of sign from the Other Side.

When Juli was 17, Colleen had a heart attack and died in her arms. The last thing Juli was able to do was squeeze her mother's hand and say, 'Mommy, I love you.' Colleen squeezed back and then she was gone.

That night, about 100 people gathered in the family home to celebrate the life of Colleen. Juli and her sister Mary were sitting on the couch. Suddenly the lights went blazing bright, then dim, then blazing bright, then dim again. Juli said, 'Mary did you see that?' Mary concurred, but no one else present had witnessed the changing lights. Juli knew that it was her mother, giving the sign she had promised. A great peace settled over her.

A decade later, Juli became engaged and made the plans for her wedding. She and her mother had talked often about the big day when Juli would marry. It grieved Juli now that her mother would not be present. The wedding was going to be a grand affair, held at the Holy Name Cathedral, the largest church in the Midwest, and with the longest aisle a bride could walk.

Two days before the wedding, Juli went to the cathedral to have a meeting with the priest. Afterwards, she approached the altar and sat in the first row. She bowed her head to pray for herself and Jim, her husband-to-be. The great church was empty, and very quiet.

As her prayer deepened, Juli became aware of a sound – a familiar sound: the click of a woman's heels on marble and the jingle of bangle bracelets. The identity was unmistakable – it was the walk of Colleen, the bracelets that always adorned her arms making music as she went.

Juli kept her head down. She thought, 'This is crazy – I must just really miss her.'

The footsteps did not go away, but came all the way from the back of the church down the long side towards Juli. Finally she looked up. The figure of a woman dressed in a raincoat who looked remarkably like her mother was beckoning to her, as if to say, 'Wait a minute, I'll get there.' In a few moments Juli was looking directly at her mother, as if she had never died, as if she were out and about on a normal day.

Colleen said, 'They told me you'd be here.' Stunned, Juli could only stammer back, 'Okay.'

'I wanted to give you something.' Colleen placed a small flat package in Juli's hands.

Juli could not tear her eyes away from her mother to look at the package. 'Are you going to be at my wedding?'

Colleen looked at her daughter lovingly and said, 'You know I would never miss your wedding. I will be there.'

Juli glanced down at the package. It was wrapped in floral gift paper. When she looked back up to say thank you, her mother had vanished. She was alone once again in the great church.

She unwrapped the present. It was a picture of Jesus with his sacred heart exposed. Colleen had always wanted Juli to be closer to God.

On the wedding day, Juli and Jim moved smoothly through the ceremony. They were praying at the altar after Mass had been said when light from one of the stained-glass windows suddenly shone on Juli's heart like a laser. It felt warm. Jim looked at her and whispered, 'It's your mom.' Juli nodded, in tears.

She had been given three miracles. Two of them came in lights – the burning and dimming lights, and the stained-glass beam. But the most amazing miracle was the picture of Jesus, which Juli still keeps among her most treasured possessions.

THE MYSTERY OF MIRACLES

What enabled these miracles to take place? Does God decide who gets a miracle and when? Are other factors involved? Does prayer make a difference? All of the cases here involved a petition to a higher power, either in a deep state of consciousness or in a quick and intense burst. And how did a door to the Other Side swing open so that Juli's mother could visit her and bring her a tangible, permanent gift?

All of these questions and more are asked whenever we participate in or witness a miracle. We wonder why some people experience miracles and others in similar circumstances do not. Is it exclusively a choice made by God, or do we ourselves play a role in determining whether or not miracles happen?

A great deal of mystery surrounds miracles. The mystery may never be completely revealed, but an examination of miracles can teach us about how and why they happen. In the following chapters, we will look at beliefs about miracles in different cultures; the role they play in religions; the meaning of personal miracles; the characteristics and mechanics of miracles; and – perhaps most significant – the innate (and largely untapped) capability in human consciousness to create miracles.

It *is* possible for us to cultivate a 'miracle mind consciousness' that encourages the miraculous to happen. Wouldn't you like to know how to bring miracles into *your* life?

CHAPTER TWO

WHAT IS
A MIRACLE?

 'I believe in miracles, but I never
thought one would happen to me.'

Almost everyone who experiences a miracle feels this way. We look at miracles as rare events that happen to others who somehow come into an unusual state of cosmic grace. We read of miraculous events in our sacred texts, and associate miracles with holiness.

And then something happens in the course of daily life that changes our perspective: an event that we can only explain as a miracle.

Kit was on her way home from her late shift at work one night, driving along a dark, two-lane road. It was about midnight, cold and wintry, and all she could think of was the pleasure of snuggling down into the warm covers of bed. Then, in the twinkling of an eye, two lives changed.

As she rounded a bend, Kit was horrified to see a pair of headlights coming straight at her on her side of the road. *God help me*, she thought. Instinctively she yanked the steering wheel, but the violent turn plus her speed sent her car careening out of control. She was only vaguely aware of the other car swerving violently, the sounds of rubber tearing at the road, and a huge crashing. She felt as though she were on the inside of a giant washing machine, being churned around. Then suddenly everything was eerily quiet, save for noises that sounded like the sparking of electrical wires.

Fortunately, Kit had been wearing a seat belt. She leaned onto the steering wheel, dazed, trying to mentally search for injuries. Her heart was pounding and she was breathing heavily. It seemed to her that somewhere nearby a fire was burning.

When she was able to collect herself, Kit looked around. The other vehicle had smashed into a telegraph pole. The front end was badly crumpled, and the car was burning. She could not see the driver. Her own car had spun off to the side nearby. She was horrified to see that it was covered with live high-voltage wires brought down by the crash. Even worse, her car was burning. There were no visible flames, but acrid smoke was beginning to waft through the interior.

With panic seizing her, Kit's first impulse was to try to jump out of the car as fast as possible. Suddenly she heard a voice, so clear and distinct it sounded as though someone was with her in the car. The voice said in a calm, matter-of-fact way, 'Do not touch the car.' Instantly Kit felt an incredible peace come over her. Later she would wonder how she could have ever felt so calm in the face of imminent death, but at this moment she felt perfectly centred and in control. The thought arose in her mind that she was safe inside the car because of the insulation of the tyres. However, because of the smoke and fire, she could not remain inside and wait for help. She somehow knew she could get out of the car, but she would have to be very careful not to touch the outside metal surface, or she would be instantly electrocuted.

Kit gingerly tried the handle of her door. The door was bent and stiff, but she was able to push it open. Carefully, with an amazing clarity and presence of mind, she slipped out, and then stepped between the tangled wires on the ground until she was able to get clear of the wreckage.

When rescuers arrived, they took her to the hospital, where it was determined that she had bruises and minor injuries. Everyone said she was extremely fortunate not to have been harmed. The other driver was not so fortunate, and perished in the accident. Others could only speculate that perhaps he had fallen asleep at the wheel and veered into Kit's lane.

For Kit, her survival of this terrifying experience was not just 'good fortune', but a miracle. It was a miracle that she had not been hit head-on and that her car had veered to relative safety. It was a miracle that she was not killed or seriously injured, or electrocuted. But the biggest miracle was the mysterious voice that told her what to do, and filled her with a calm certainty that everything was going to be all right. She had no idea how she'd 'known' that the car was insulated by its tyres.

'It could only have been the voice of God,' said Kit. 'I never really thought about miracles happening to me, but if this wasn't a miracle, I don't know what is. I asked God to help me, and he did.'

DEFINING MIRACLES

Exactly what is a miracle? Is it a natural event or a supernatural one? Is it strictly of divine origin?

The word 'miracle' comes from the Latin term *miraculum*, which derives from mirari, or 'to wonder'. Miracles are 'wonderful things'. Defining them beyond that is not a simple task. In fact, there is no one, all-encompassing definition of a miracle. Rather, the meaning of what is miraculous is shaded by perspective and world-view. There are differences between Western and Eastern ideas of what constitutes a miracle.

Western Views

To most Westerners, a miracle is an event that has no natural explanation according to the known laws of science and nature. Without a natural explanation, miracles can only then be possible by divine intervention: the reaching out of the hand of God.

Miracles play an important role in Judaism and Christianity. Both religions trace their origins to events viewed as both historical and miraculous: the Exodus of the Jews from Egypt in Judaism, and the Resurrection of Jesus in Christianity. Of all the great religions, Christianity, especially in the Catholic tradition, has developed the most systematic account of miracles.

In the Judaeo-Christian traditions, miracles are seen specifically as acts of God that signal his presence in the world and demonstrate his covenant with humanity. As creator of the world, it is expected that God will intervene in it when it suits his purpose.

There is no Hebrew word equivalent to 'miracle'. The Old Testament tells many stories of 'signs and wonders' by which God reveals his intentions. They are almost all public events witnessed by many, and are executed directly by God or by certain prophets of great holiness.

The most important wonder-worker of the Old Testament is Moses. God speaks to him initially through a burning bush. The book of Exodus, the liberation of the Israelites from captivity in Egypt, is full of miracles performed by Moses and also his brother Aaron. They turn their staffs into snakes to defeat the magicians of the pharaoh. They turn the waters of the Nile into blood. Moses brings on plagues to force the pharaoh to set his people free. In the Exodus, he parts the waters of the Red Sea.

Perhaps most dramatic is the miracle of the revelation of the Ten Commandments directly to Moses on Mount Sinai, amidst a formidable display of the elements. The people are awe-struck by thunder, lightning, smoke, fire and blasts of a divine trumpet. Moses speaks and God answers him in thunder.

Other Old Testament prophets also are wonder-workers acting under the instructions of God. Joshua is instrumental in bringing down the walls of Jericho. On another occasion, during a battle, he causes hail-stones to rain down on the enemies, and the sun and moon to stand still. Elijah multiplies food and restores a dead child to life, and cheats death and ascends directly to heaven.

In the New Testament the central wonder-worker is Jesus, born of a miraculous virgin conception, who performs public and personal miracles. Among them are numerous healings by word and touch, and the casting out of demons. At a gathering of five thousand people, he multiplies a few fishes and loaves of bread to feed to the entire crowd. He walks on water and shows his disciple Peter how to do it; but Peter's fear causes him to sink. Jesus turns water into wine and raises the dead. Lazarus has been dead three days when Jesus calls him forth from his tomb. The greatest miracle of Jesus is his resurrection from the dead by God and his ascent into heaven.

Jesus performed his miracles to demonstrate the power of God in the world, and also to show that this power flows through all of us, if we but have the faith to accept it and use it. 'According to your faith, be it done to you,' he is quoted in Matthew 9:29. And, 'He who believes in me will also do the works that I do; and greater works than these will he do,' he is quoted in John 14:12.

Following his resurrection, his apostles take up wonder-working as a way of spreading the gospel. The masses, however, do not take the mantle from them. The role of wonder-working is left to the holy.

Both Judaism and Christianity have strong traditions of miracles performed by holy people. In Judaism, rabbis, sages, rebbes (itinerant preachers) and other pious people perform miracles as a result of leading righteous lives.

In Catholic Christianity, saints are the primary wonder-workers, able to perform their miracles because of their purity and holiness. Saints act as intercessors who form a bridge between humanity and the awesomeness of God. Their relics – their body parts, clothing and personal belongings, as well as objects that come into contact with relics – become imbued with a mediating power for the manifestation of miracles. More about the miracles of saints will be explored in the next chapter.

Protestantism rejects the community of saints, but allows for miracles to be performed both by God and certain persons whose holiness enables them to channel the power of God: evangelists, preachers and spiritual healers.

Western religions accept the idea of a natural order of things and laws of nature, which are considered the work of God, and hold that God can suspend or otherwise intervene in the natural order. Miracles always have a religious purpose. The New Testament miracles are presented as providing a divine sanction of the person

and message of Christ. This stress on the meaning of the
miracle sets the Judaeo-Christian concept of miracle
apart from miracle stories in other religious traditions.
Miracles occur not because they can, but because God
manifests them specifically for the purpose of teaching
and demonstration.

Eastern Views

To someone from the Eastern part of the world, miracles
are seen differently. They are part of the natural world –
simply the way things are. The gods of Hinduism, however, do perform miracles as a way of intervening in the
affairs of people. The most significant of these is
Krishna, an *avatar* (incarnation) of the creator god,
Vishnu, who descends into human form in order to
battle the forces of chaos. His miracles have the two-
fold purpose of maintaining the right order of things,
and also inspiring human faith and devotion. He

successfully battles demons and lifts a mountain aloft for seven days and nights.

Like Jesus, Buddha has a miraculous birth: he enters his mother in a dream in which her belly is pierced by a sacred elephant. Inside he has a special enclosure that protects him from the taint of flesh, and he emerges from his mother's right side possessing full memory and knowledge. Seven days later, his mother dies.

Buddha develops miraculous abilities in the course of his spiritual development. These are considered a natural part of the spiritualization process. As he instructs his disciples, miracles are not to be performed for vanity or gain, or for their own sake. To do so is to show that you are still attached to the material world.

In Eastern traditions, stories abound of holy persons who perform miracles similar to those of Western saints and holy ones.

Miracles through Yoga

The way of yoga enables a person to become god-like. Most Westerners are familiar with only one school of yoga, hatha yoga, which features breathing techniques and body stretches and postures. Yoga is much more complex, and consists of different schools of practices that involve meditation, mental disciplines and the training of consciousness to experience union with the Absolute. Along the way, one naturally acquires miraculous abilities and powers. The Eastern adept strives to get past them. Miraculous abilities are distractions on the path to union with the Absolute.

Miraculous powers are called *siddhi* in Sanskrit, which means 'perfect abilities' and 'miraculous powers'. According to the Yoga Sutra of Patanjali, the *siddhi* include such abilities as: clairvoyance (the ability to know the mental states of others); knowledge of one's previous lives; levitation; miraculous transport (covering great distances in an instant); knowledge of and control over all bodily functions; shrinking and expanding the body; rendering oneself and other things invisible; projecting one's consciousness out-of-body; projecting one's consciousness into another body; possessing superhuman strength; knowledge of all languages; knowledge of the sounds of animals; and knowledge of the moment when one will die.

The Buddhist traditions of yoga are similar. The extraordinary powers are called *iddhi* in Pali, meaning 'wondrous gifts'. The *iddhi* are the eight powers of mastery over the body and nature: invincibility, invisibility, fleetness in running, ability to see the gods, control over spirits and demons, the ability to fly, the preservation of youth, and the ability to make certain pills (such as for immortality).

The development of the *iddhi* is not considered harmful, but it is not encouraged, either. The *iddhi* are potential pitfalls that will turn the student away from the path to enlightenment. Attitudes towards *iddhi* have varied among schools of Buddhism. Shakyamuni Buddha, the historical Buddha, forbade the use and display of *iddhi*, especially to people who were not initiates. The same powers are possible through the use of magic – the manipulation of natural forces – and thus might not be a true demonstration of spiritual transformation. Some schools of Buddhism have continued that tradition.

One of the most famous adepts of Tibetan Buddhism was Milarepa, who lived from 1052–1135. According to tradition, Milarepa learned black magical arts and then renounced them in favour of a spiritual path. He undertook intense training in yoga and developed the *iddhi*. He was witnessed flying. He travelled out-of-body at will, not only anywhere on earth, but also to other planes and worlds, where he would hold discussions with spiritual masters. He could shape-shift into a flame, bird or running stream. Others wanted him to teach the powers in order to use them for material gain, but Milarepa stayed focused on his spiritual teachings.

Sathya Sai Baba

In India, Sathya Sai Baba is regarded as a living avatar, an incarnation of God. His *siddhi* feats have attracted a huge following of devotees around the world. Sai Baba is renowned for his healing; his apports, or materializations of precious gems, jewellery, devotional objects and even hot foods and liquids; bilocation; mystical transport, or teleportation; levitation; precognition and luminous phenomena.

He was born in 1926 as Sathyanarayana Ratnakara Raju.(Sathya means 'truth' and Narayana is a name for God). He began exhibiting miraculous gifts in his teens after being stung by a black scorpion. He lapsed into a coma for several hours and awoke a different person. He would fall into trances from which he could not be roused, and would offer sudden discourses on ancient Hindu philosophy. He would suddenly sing and recite poetry.

On 23 May 1940, shortly after the scorpion incident, he left school and announced to his family that he was the reborn Sai Baba. Sai is a Muslim term for 'saint' and Baba is a Hindi term of respect for 'father'. The original Sai Baba had been a middle-class Brahmin fakir of the turn of the century, who had settled in Shirdi, about 120 miles north-east of Bombay, and had produced astounding miracles. Now reborn, he materialized for his parents flowers, sugar candy and rice cooked in milk, all with a wave of his hand.

Although he quickly attracted devotees, not everyone loved him, and some denounced him as a fraud. For decades, Sai Baba has used his miraculous abilities and has not been detected of fraud, even when studied by Western psychical researchers, albeit on a restricted basis.

Sai Baba materializes huge quantities of *vibuti*, holy ash made from burnt cow dung, which is smeared on the body; foods and liquids; religious statues and objects made of gold; precious jewellery; photographs; business cards; even stamps bearing his likeness, which have not been officially issued by the government. He reportedly fills empty bowls with hot, steaming Indian food of most unusual flavours, and produces enough to feed hundreds of people at a time. He opens his fist and drops sticky sweets into the palms of others, yet his own hands are dry. He also produces *amrith*, a honey-like substance. He has reached into sand and pulled out food free of sand. He has plucked apples, pomegranates, mangoes and other fruits from a tamarind tree. All non-food objects materialized are bright, fresh and new. Jewellery includes valuable precious gems. Rings requested by followers fit them perfectly; if a person does not like a particular ring, Sai Baba takes it back and changes it instantly. Business cards bearing his name appear to be freshly printed. Many objects are inscribed with his name.

In his earlier days, he frequently fell into sudden, often convulsive, trances which lasted up to one-and-a-half days, and during which his body would be very cold to the touch. His explanation was that he had been called to another, often distant, location to help people in distress or illness. In these other locations, he reportedly appeared as if in the flesh. If he had gone out of body to heal, he sometimes would return showing symptoms of the illness. People who prayed to him for healing reported miraculous recoveries, and sometimes said he visited them in their dreams or came to their bedside.

In one reported instance during a trance, Sai Baba levitated. While in the air, the sole of his right foot split open, and an estimated two kilograms of *vibuti* poured out. In another trance incident, he opened his mouth and out fell *vibuti* and golden plates a half-inch in width. One of the plates was inscribed in Telugu, 'Sri Rama'.

Sai Baba would also appear to teleport himself up a hill, disappearing at its base and appearing at the top of the hill within seconds. From the hilltop, he would produce luminosities so brilliant and blinding that others had to shade their eyes. Some witnesses collapsed from the brightness.

Other phenomena attributed to him include: the instant changing of the colour of his loose robes; weather control; unusual smells, often produced at a distance; the appearance of *vibuti* and *amrith* on pictures of him and on his apports; psychic surgery; the changing of water into other beverages and into petrol; mind reading; and clairvoyance. Some of those who touched him experienced a mild electrical shock. Once, he was found to have a nest of scorpions living in his bushy hair. During his early days, he forbade photographs and films to be taken of him. Those who attempted to do so surreptitiously found their film to be blank when developed.

In 1973, a prominent psychical researcher, Dr Erlendur Haraldsson, a psychologist from the University of Iceland, began a 10-year investigation of Sai Baba. He was aided by Dr Karlis Osis of the American Society for Psychical Research, Dr Michael Thalbourne of Washington University and Dr Joop Houtkooper of the University of Amsterdam. Sai Baba declined to submit to controlled experiments, but it was possible for the researchers to observe him closely on many occasions. They witnessed him materialize up to 40 objects a day. When he waved his hand to produce *vibuti*, it seemed to appear in the air just below his palm.

The conclusion of the researchers is that they found no evidence to disprove the phenomena – thus reinforcing the devotees' faith that Sai Baba truly is an incarnation of God and a performer of miracles.

Islam and the Sufi Tradition

Islam, which was influenced by Christianity, has both Western and Eastern views about miracles. Islam acknowledges miracles as signs of the presence and action of Allah in the world. The prophet Muhammad refused to perform them, however, reminding his followers that all things, being made by Allah, are signs of His power and goodness. Nonetheless, miracle stories are recounted of Sufi holy men, and some of the orders are known for extraordinary achievements, such as swallowing coals. Sufi saints perform miracles as a way of teaching people about spirituality. Some masters reject miracles as magical acts or tricks and teach that true mystics pursue a higher path.

Miracles in Other Traditions

In pantheistic religions, the divine is not separate from the world of nature. Miraculous events are part of the broad spectrum of things that exist in the natural world. Access to that part of the natural world requires special skill or training, such as in shamanism. The shaman learns how to alter consciousness in order to perform miraculous tasks like those performed by saints and holy persons in other spiritual traditions.

The shaman has the power to see spirits and souls, and to communicate with them – to know the language of other creatures. He is able to take magical-mystical flights to the heavens, where he can serve as an intermediary between the gods and the people; he can descend to the underworld to the land of the dead. The flights are done by shape-shifting, by riding mythical horses or the spirits of sacrificed horses or by travelling in spirit boats.

The shaman's primary function is to heal and restore the individual's connection to the universe. Shamans make no distinction between body, mind and spirit; they are all part of the whole. Another important function is control of the elements, especially the ability to make rain, for the life of the community may depend upon it. Shamans also prophesy.

Miracles versus Magic

Magic is an art or process that can produce the same things as miracles. Few people, however, consider magic to be an act or a grace of God. We perceive miracles as happening when they need to, at God's discretion. We consider magic as something humans try to do themselves to bend the laws of nature according to their own will.

The difference between miracles and magic often boils down to one's perspective. In the Bible, the supernatural feats performed by the prophets are miracles, but when the same feats are done by those who worship other gods they are called magic. In the stories, the miracles of God always triumph over the magic of the heathen gods.

As we saw earlier, Moses and Aaron follow God's instructions to 'perform all the wonders' he has empowered them to do in front of the pharaoh, in order to persuade the ruler to release the Israelites. Exodus tells how Aaron throws down his staff and it becomes a snake. The pharaoh summons his wise men and sorcerers. 'They also, the magicians of Egypt, did the same by their secret arts.

Each one threw down his staff, and they became snakes; but Aaron's staff swallowed up theirs' (Exodus 7:11–12).

The simplest definition of magic is that it is the art of effecting change with the help of higher forces. Higher forces can include spirit beings, such as angels; intercessory figures such as saints; God; Goddess; and a host of personifications of the Godhead represented by various deities. Higher forces also include the inner powers within us: intuition; guidance from the Higher Self; will and determination; the creative power of thought and belief; and, most important of all, the power of love, which brings everything into balance.

The awareness of magic and the use of it to enhance life are ancient and universal. The earliest evidence of magic dates to cave paintings of the Palaeolithic Age, some of which suggest magic rituals were employed to secure successful hunts. Various magical systems and philosophies have developed around the world, and volumes of literature have been written on them.

The term 'magic' comes either from the Greek *megus*, which means 'great' (as in 'great' science), or from the Greek term *magein*, for the science and religion of Zoroaster of ancient Persia. Numerous definitions of magic have been offered by many who have practised and studied it, yet magic eludes precise description. Many systems of magic exist, and some are quite complex and secret. Generally, 'low magic' is spell-casting and 'high magic' involves working with the higher planes of consciousness and spiritual beings. The magician actively works to bring about a desired change.

Miracles and magic are facets of the movement of cosmic power. Our personal, cultural and religious beliefs give us a framework for relating to this power. Attitudes shift with time. For example, 19th-century cultural anthropologists tended to classify all claims of miraculous events under the heading of magic.

Modern Personal Views of Miracles

In modern Western culture, miracles have acquired a wider popular definition than found in religious thought. A miracle is any unlikely, unusual or unexplained event that has a significant impact on life. They do not need to happen on a grand scale, such as the parting of the Red Sea by Moses. Miracles can happen quietly and be intensely personal. In fact, most modern miracles are likely to be personal and not public. Most involve healing – any prayer service or circle receives more prayers for miraculous healing than any other situation.

A personal miracle occurs any time life takes an unexpected turn and a crisis or disaster is avoided, or fortunes suddenly improve in unforeseen ways.

Let's go deeper into miracles. We'll look first at religious miracles, for they form the foundations of our traditional beliefs about miracles.

CHAPTER THREE

THE MIRACLES
OF SAINTS

 In 1998, a 17-month-old boy, Robert Gutherman, who had been born with nerve deafness, was determined to have been miraculously cured of his affliction in his right ear.

Two years later, a seven-year-old girl, Amanda Wall, was miraculously cured of nerve deafness in both ears. Both cases had one thing in common: the families of the children had prayed to Blessed Katharine Drexel, a holy woman of the Catholic Church who died in 1955. Amanda's family began praying to Katharine after hearing about the Robert Gutherman case. They also obtained objects that had belonged to Katharine and had touched Amanda's ears with them. Within five months, changes were noticed in the girl's responses. Medical tests confirmed she had normal hearing in both ears.

The miraculous healings were attributed to the intercession of Katharine. The Vatican agreed, and on 1 October 2000, Katharine Drexel was canonized by Pope John Paul II, becoming the second American-born person to join the prestigious ranks of sainthood. During her life (1858–1955), the Philadelphia-born heiress to a railroad fortune had used her wealth to help the poor, especially Native Americans and African Americans. She founded the Sisters of the Blessed Sacrament, and built schools and missions.

People sought her help while she was alive. After her death, they prayed to her in the faith that she could help them have their prayers answered. Her cause for sainthood was advanced, and she was beatified in 1988.

St Katharine Drexel is but one of thousands of holy figures in the history of Christianity. Some have been proclaimed saints by popular accord; others have been proclaimed saints by the official process of canonization established by the Catholic Church.

The lives of the saints are filled with stories of miracles. Many are a mix of fact and legend, especially of men and women in the early Church, but many nonetheless have been established as reliable accounts. Many of the stories are awe-inspiring. The Church may value saints for their charitable works, piety and sanctity, and contributions to theology and doctrine, but the populace values and reveres saints for their miracle-making powers – their ability to make a difference in the life of an individual.

So powerful is our collective belief in the miraculous powers of saints that we look to them in time of need regardless of our particular religious creeds. When a depression occurred in the American housing market during the 1980s, people faced difficulties selling their homes. Houses sat and sat on the market. Stories began appearing in the media that sellers who had buried a stature of St Jude in their gardens had then quickly sold their homes, even if the properties had been languishing on the market for months. Suddenly statues of St Jude – the patron saint of hopeless causes – were all the rage. 'I can't explain how or why it works, but it does,' attested successful sellers, not all of whom were Catholic, or even Christian, or even of any particular religious bent.

Why are saints especially graced with miraculous abilities? In Christian tradition, a life dedicated to the selfless love of, and service to, God opens the way for the power of miracles to flow through that person as divine grace. Jesus set the model with his miracles, and declared that others could do the same.

St Paul, writing in one of his letters to the Corinthians, established that the gifts of the Holy Spirit were dispensed by God:

> To one, indeed, by the Spirit, is given the word of wisdom: and to another the word of knowledge, according to the same Spirit; to another, faith in the same spirit; to another the grace of healing in one Spirit; to another, the working of miracles; to another, prophecy; to another, the discerning of spirits; to another, diverse kinds of tongues; to another, interpretation of speeches. But all these things one and the same Spirit worketh, dividing to everyone according as he will. (1 Cor. 12:8–11)

The idea that everyone could perform miracles never took hold in popular consciousness, however; miracles became the province of the especially holy. In Christianity, miracle-making always serves a purpose: to convert, and to inspire the faithful to a greater love of God. Many of the early monks and evangelists were famous for their control of the elements and of animals, their healing ability, their ability to manifest food and water, and their uncanny ability to know the secret thoughts of others. There are numerous stories of holy men striking barren, dry ground with their staffs, and springs of water – usually with healing properties – gushing forth. After their death, more miracles were reported by the faithful who visited their tombs and prayed to them for intercessory help.

THE EVOLUTION OF SAINTHOOD

Saintly people have been important to Christianity from its earliest days. At worship services, their names were read from honour rolls, and they were remembered, invoked and prayed to. Initially, the lists of the holy were mostly martyrs who died for their faith. Martyrs were joined by other figures – monks, abbots and evangelists – who had led distinguished lives. These lists, or canons, became the basis for the process of canonization. Over time the lists were augmented with calendars.

By the seventh century, the first formal procedures for the veneration of deceased holy persons were developed. Veneration had to be approved by a local bishop or a provincial or national council. Candidates were evaluated based on their lives, teachings, writings, works of charity, virtues and sanctity, and miraculous feats.

In the 10th century, the Holy See – the central authority of the Church – became involved in veneration. The first formal canonization took place in 993 when Pope John XV conferred sainthood upon Udalric, the bishop of Augsburg. The papacy became increasingly involved in canonization. In 1234, Pope Gregory IX established that the papacy would have complete jurisdiction over the process. Canonization evolved into a formal procedure.

In 1983, significant changes were made in the process of canonization by Pope John Paul II. The cause of beatification, the first step, is initiated after the death of a candidate. Often the followers of the candidate want the process to begin immediately, but years may elapse first. This waiting period is beneficial, in that it allows for a more objective perspective. Of foremost importance is not miracle-making, but the holiness and sanctity of the candidate. His or her life, writings and works (or martyrdom) are investigated locally by the bishop for heroic virtue and orthodoxy of doctrine. The investigation is evaluated by a panel of theologians at the Vatican. If the candidate has lived a life of faith and morals and is approved by the panel and by the Congregation for the Causes of Saints, the pope proclaims the candidate 'Venerable'.

The next step is beatification. Miracles become important – but they must be posthumous miracles, not deeds done during life. There must be proof of at least one posthumous miracle that results from a petition (martyrs are excepted from this requirement). The miracle establishes that the candidate is in heaven and has the ability to intercede on behalf of the living, and to mediate a divine intervention that cannot be explained according to the laws of science. First, all the evidence for the miracle is gathered, including historical, clinical and depositions of witnesses. The evidence is critically studied. A 'Positio', a volume of documentation, is written. If the miracle involved a physical event such as a healing, the Positio is reviewed by a medical board of specialists. The case is assessed by a board of theologians, and evaluated at a meeting of cardinals and bishops who are members of the Congregation for the Causes of Saints.

If the miracle can be proved and the cause goes forward, the pope proclaims the candidate 'Blessed' (*Beatus*), which means he or she can be venerated in localities or by groups of people to whom they have an importance.

For canonization, in which the candidate is proclaimed 'Saint', a second posthumous miracle is required. This requirement applies to martyrs, too. The same process as for beatification is followed. Saints are 'raised to the altars', that is, they are venerated by the entire Church and given feast days observed throughout the entire Church.

The Church considers saints to be the servants of God and stresses that it does not 'make' saints, but rather recognizes the holiness in them, and that they are in heaven and can intercede on behalf of those who petition them. And when people petition saints, they are often praying for a miracle.

Below are examples of how miracles manifested in the lives of saints.

Beloved Francis

Francis of Assisi (1181?–1226) is one of the most beloved saints around the world. He is described as the most Christ-like of all the saints. He is especially known for his love of animals, his miracles and for his stigmata (wounds that imitate the wounds of the crucifixion), said to be given to him by an angel. He is considered to be the founder of all Franciscan orders.

As a young man, Francis enjoyed the good life, spending his father's money and indulging himself. But during an illness he had a miracle – either a visionary dream or an auditory experience of the direct voice of God – in which God instructed him to 'serve the master and not the man'.

He began visiting the sick and poor, giving them whatever he had. He spent more time in prayer, even removing himself to a cave, where he wept and prayed about his sins. He sold his father's horse to get money to rebuild a ruined church. His father was outraged. Francis stuck to his new religious life, and attracted a band of followers. They became travelling preachers.

In 1224, aged 42, he had an ecstatic vision during a long fast and prayer vigil on the suffering of Jesus. A seraph, a six-winged angel, descended from heaven and revealed the crucified Jesus within the folds of its fiery wings. When the vision ended, Francis's hands and feet were marked with black excrescences in the form of nail heads and bent nails, and a wound oozing blood formed on his side. The marks and the bleeding wound remained for the last two years of his life. He kept them hidden from others.

Francis had miraculous abilities. He understood the language of animals and demonstrated a remarkable rapport with them. They would gather around him when he preached. He multiplied food on more than one occasion. Once, when a priest complained that followers of Francis were eating too many of the church's grapes,

Francis said that they should be allowed to do so, and the vineyard would produce more wine than normal. He also multiplied food when a ship he was travelling in was wrecked.

According to one story, he influenced the weather, ending frequent hailstorms that were destroying crops. Francis told the people to confess their sins and repent. The hailstorms ended. The people, however, eventually went back to their old ways, and were struck by pestilence and a fire that destroyed their town. St Francis also performed miracle healings. All these miraculous abilities manifested when he gave up his material ways and dedicated himself to God.

The Amazing Padre Pio

Another of the most beloved modern saints is Blessed Padre Pio (1887–1968), a Capuchin friar from southern Italy. Padre Pio experienced numerous mystical experiences and had miraculous gifts. He was especially renowned for his stigmata, and for his bilocation, the ability to be in two distant places simultaneously.

In his youth, Padre Pio suffered from tuberculosis. He spent most of his life in the monastery of San Giovanni Rotondo. In 1910, bloodless, half-inch wounds appeared in the middle of his hands. They remained for several days and then disappeared after prayer. The wounds appeared intermittently for the next eight years.

On 20 September 1918, Padre Pio was kneeling in front of a large crucifix in the church when he received the stigmata. He was the first priest in the history of the Church to receive fully the five wounds of Christ, not just marks. Doctors examined him but could find no natural causes. His tuberculosis disappeared at this time.

Padre Pio had the stigmata throughout his life. The wounds bled constantly and the blood was sweetly perfumed with roses and violets. He was unable to close his hands because of the wounds, and was required to wear gloves at all times except during Mass. He wore special shoes to cover the wounds on his feet. Padre Pio's stigmata were the longest on record. Other stigmatists experienced their wounds on certain days, or for certain durations. He accurately predicted that upon his death the wounds would completely heal.

The stigmata ignited Padre Pio's popularity and people flocked to see him. Church officials were not pleased, however, and in 1923 he was silenced. He was forbidden to write letters and to preach, but could say Mass and hear confessions. The silencing failed to dampen public ardour, and appointments for confessions had to be made far in advance.

On 9 January 1940, he established the Home for the Relief of Suffering, which was dedicated on 5 May 1956. With donations he created a hospital open to anyone who appealed for assistance and love in the name of Christ.

Padre Pio died on 23 January 1968. He was considered a saint long before he died. Thousands came to pay their respects, and more than 100,000 people attended his burial on 26 September. Tradition holds that he gave off a sweet fragrance as he was placed in his tomb. In 1999, Pope John Paul II beatified him.

Padre Pio had the gift of many miraculous abilities and acts, which attracted to him many devotees. His prophecies were accurate. He performed miracle healings. In one case, a mother with a seriously ill infant boy decided to bring him to Padre Pio in the hope of a cure. But during the journey to the monastery, the baby died. The desperate mother wrapped up the body and put it in a suitcase. When she arrived at the church, Padre Pio was hearing confessions. She waited in line, and when her turn came, she dumped out the body of her son, sobbing in great grief. Padre Pio was horrified and prayed. He then turned to the mother and said, 'Why are you crying so loud? Can't you see that your son is sleeping?' Miraculously, the baby was alive and was asleep.

A girl who was born with no pupils in her eyes was brought to Padre Pio. He made the sign of the cross over her eyes, and miraculously she could see. Her vision stayed with her the rest of her life.

Padre Pio was known to bilocate on numerous occasions. Many of his bilocations were to perform miraculous healing, in response to the numerous prayers made to him for his intercession. He bilocated all over the world. In one case, a woman in Genoa was in danger of losing her leg to amputation. One of her daughters prayed intensely to Padre Pio, who was hundreds of miles away at his monastery. Suddenly the daughter saw him standing in the doorway of her room. He told her to wait for nine days, and vanished. The daughter was able to prevail upon the doctors, and no operation was performed. On the 10th day, the mother's leg was completely healed.

Padre Pio seemed to be consciously aware of his bilocations. Once a young English couple appealed by letter to Padre Pio for help with their problems. They received no answer, and so scraped together enough money to travel to the monastery. In Berne, Switzerland, they spent the night in a cheap inn. They could afford only the attic, which was damp, mouldy and cold. Furthermore, it was winter, and the snow was heavy. Discouraged, they thought about turning back. After all, they could arrive at San Giovanni Rotondo and never get to see Padre Pio. Suddenly a sweet perfume filled the room. They had no idea where it came from – nor could the innkeeper explain it – but it comforted them. They decided to continue on to Italy.

At the monastery, Padre Pio greeted them like old friends. Perplexed, they said he had not even answered their letter. 'What do you mean, I did not reply?' said Padre Pio. 'I replied that night at the inn. Did you not smell the perfume?' He helped them solve their problems, and they returned home to England happy.

Padre Pio had a constant and close relationship with his guardian angel. He believed that God used the angel to make it possible for him to understand foreign languages he had not learned, and to have clairvoyant knowledge of secrets within the heart (especially useful to him during confessions). Padre Pio would tell people that whenever they were in need of his prayer, to address his guardian angel through their guardian angels. Once a busload of pilgrims, en route to San Giovanni Rotondo, got caught at night in a violent lightning storm in the Apennine mountains. They followed Padre Pio's advice, and weathered the storm unscathed. When they arrived the next day, and before they could tell their story, Pio announced that he had been awakened by his guardian angel during the night, and had prayed for them.

It is easy to see why millions of people around the world have adopted Padre Pio as their patron saint.

A Trans-Atlantic Traveller

Padre Pio may be famous for his bilocations, but the record-holder probably is Venerable Mary of Agreda (1602–65). Born in Agreda, Spain, to a religious family, Mary entered the Convent of the Immaculate Conception for discalced (shoeless) nuns at the age of 17. She became abbess when she was 25.

Mary experienced numerous bilocations, as well as ecstasies, levitations and other mystical and miraculous phenomena. During her ecstasies, her body was raised off the ground and could be moved as weightlessly as a feather. Her face was enraptured in beauty. She would remain in trances for two to three hours at a time.

Mary bilocated spontaneously and travelled mystically throughout Spain and Portugal. From 1620–31, she travelled to America to teach the Indians. She made more than 500 visits, sometimes as many as four a day. The natives called her the Lady in Blue because of her blue mantle. She appeared in New Mexico and reached an isolated tribe. She spoke in her native Spanish, but was miraculously understood by the Indians. She gave them Christian instruction and also directions for where to go in New Mexico and Texas to find Christian missions. Mary said she was commanded to do this travelling to America by Jesus.

From 1627–37, the Blessed Virgin Mary appeared to her while she was in ecstasies and commanded her to write the Blessed Virgin's life. In her visions, Mary ascended a ladder and went through a portal to heaven, where she was greeted by the Lord of Hosts and the Blessed Virgin. Mary resisted writing about her visionary experiences until 1637, when she began to set down what became *The Mystical City of God*, a four-volume, 2,676-page history of the Blessed Virgin's life, Jesus and his hidden life, the creation of the world, the Apocalypse, heaven and hell and other Christian topics.

Flying Saints

Reports of levitating saints abound in the literature of saints. Numerous saints have been witnessed to levitate off the ground, some at considerable height, and even remain suspended in the air for prolonged periods. The levitations have usually occurred during periods of intense prayer or states of rapture.

Probably the most famous levitating saint of Christianity is Joseph of Cupertino (1603–63), a Franciscan mystic from Cupertino, Italy, who had a difficult time staying on the ground. As a child, Joseph was dull and went about with his mouth hanging open, which earned him the nickname of 'the Gaper'. He had a bad temper. At the age of eight, he had his first ecstatic vision. His open mouth probably was the result of his frequent visions.

Joseph desperately wanted to join a religious order, but was rejected by two of them because of his lack of education and his inability to function due to his frequent ecstasies. Finally, he was taken in as a lay brother by the Franciscans at La Grotella near Cupertino. He was assigned to work in the stables. There his disposition improved and in 1628 he was ordained as a priest.

Joseph's life was comprised of visions and mystical experiences. Almost anything holy would trigger an ecstatic experience. The name of God, Mary or a saint; the tolling of a church bell; church music; sacred images; and even thoughts about sacred things would send Joseph into another state of consciousness and off the ground. He was especially prone to mystical experience during Mass. During his trances, he did not respond to any stimuli, even the piercing of his flesh with needles or the dragging about of his body. Only the voice of his superior would affect him.

Joseph became famous for his spectacular levitations and aerial flights. He would rise several feet into the air, sometimes enraptured by the sound of heavenly music that only he could hear. He would fly about over the heads of others and remain suspended in the air for long periods of time. He flew up to holy statues and to altars. Whenever he rose into the air, he would give out a shriek of ecstasy. The total number of his levitations is not known; more than 70 were recorded during his early years at La Grotella alone.

His flights happened both indoors and outdoors. Once he saw a lamb in a friary garden and went into a rapture over the Lamb of God, rising into the air with the lamb in his arms. After hearing a priest say, 'Father Joseph, how beautiful God has made heaven,' he flew up to a branch on an olive tree and knelt on the branch for half an hour, bending it no more than would a small bird.

In 1644, he amazed the Spanish ambassador to the Papal Court, his wife and attendants by flying over their heads to a statue of Mary in church. The ambassador's wife fainted and had to be revived with smelling salts.

When he visited Pope Urban VIII in Rome, he kissed the pontiff's feet and rose spontaneously into the air. The amazed pope said that if Joseph died before he did, he would attest to the miracle himself.

Unfortunately for Joseph, his levitations hindered his life. His peers were so annoyed by the disruptions and the crowds he attracted that eventually he was restricted to his private room. He was not allowed to participate in devotions and worship, or even to eat with his fellow friars. His enemies reported him to the Inquisition. He levitated before astonished inquisitors in 1653. The inquisitors could find no demonic fault with him, but for the rest of his life, he was held a virtual prisoner in a succession of remote monasteries. Nobody wanted him.

Other miraculous powers and abilities were attributed to Joseph. He could bilocate. He was prophetic and had numerous accurate visions of the future. He could read the minds and hearts of others, and knew their secret, unconfessed sins. He could control the elements and stop storms. He had command over animals, even greater than that of St Francis of Assisi. He exuded a sweet perfume that clung to everything he used, and permeated the rooms he entered. He could detect the stench of sin, a terrible odour not detectable by ordinary people, that surrounded those who were leading sinful or evil lives.

There were so many witnessed accounts of Joseph's levitations and flying that it is hard to dismiss them as legend built up to glorify a saint, especially since the feats were more of a liability to him than an asset.

THE MEANING OF SAINTLY MIRACLES

What levitation and other miracles of the saints demonstrate is that when we are in a certain state of consciousness, the natural laws are transcended, and we are capable of things we call miraculous. The same applies to other miraculous powers exhibited by holy persons.

They are able to attain, and even sustain, a state of consciousness profoundly different from what we call 'ordinary' consciousness. For them, this is achieved through intense spiritual practice. For an 'ordinary' person, this state of consciousness happens spontaneously, often in response to an immediate and urgent need. Learning more about miracles will help us understand how to cultivate the right state of consciousness that is conducive to miracles. To do it, you needn't withdraw to a monastery. You can do it as a part of daily life.

Before we leave the realm of the saints, let's look at more miraculous powers associated with them: relics, holy objects and holy places.

CHAPTER FOUR

MIRACULOUS RELICS, PLACES AND OBJECTS

Throughout history we have not only venerated the person and memory of the holy, but also their relics: preserved body parts, bits of bone, clothing and belongings.

Owning or touching a relic puts us in touch with the power of the holy person, and thus miracles may happen. We also follow the ancient custom of making pilgrimages to special places in search of miracles, especially healing. Shrines where saints are buried or their relics are kept are power points for miraculous intercessory help.

RELICS

Veneration of relics is found throughout the world. Relics of Buddha, including his teeth, hairs and some body parts, are enshrined in towers called *stupas*. Two hairs of Muhammad are preserved in a domed temple in Jerusalem. In Christianity, the most prized relics are those of Jesus. There are no physical remains, of course, but pieces of his cross, his crown of thorns, and things relating to his crucifixion have been highly prized. Relics of the Blessed Virgin Mary, including clothing, furnishings and her shroud, also are highly prized.

The veneration of relics of the saints was well established by the fourth century, and was at its peak during the Middle Ages. Relics remain popular today. Great care is taken to preserve relics in ornate containers called reliquaries, made of gold, silver and crystal and sometimes encrusted with precious gems, in which they are exposed to the veneration of the faithful. So important are relics that the bodies of some saints have been partially dismembered so that their remains could be dispersed to various congregations. For example, numerous relics were taken from the incorrupt body of St Francis Xavier (1506–52), popular Jesuit missionary from Spain. In 1949, his severed arm was toured throughout Japan and the United States to commemorate the 400th anniversary of Francis's arrival in Japan.

Do relics possess a miraculous or magical power? Objects do seem to absorb the essences of their owners. For example, a psychically sensitive person can hold an object and 'read' information about its owner. This is called psychometry, a term that refers to the 'soul of things'.

Thus, the physical remains and possessions of a saint can be seen to retain the saint's essence, and provide a person with a link to the saint in heaven for the purpose of intercession. Remember how the family of the deaf girl, Amanda Wall, held objects belonging to St Katharine Drexel to the girl's ears as part of their petition to the saint. There are numerous cases of similar miraculous healings involving holy objects.

The Church is careful to distinguish the veneration of relics from connotations of 'magic'. Relics do provide a spiritual link to a saint, but not through any intrinsic power of their own. The Vatican II Council stated that veneration of relics is part of the traditional honouring of saints: 'For the feasts of the saints proclaim the wonderful works of Christ in His servants, and display to the faithful fitting examples for their imitation.' Nonetheless, relics are perceived as powerful objects, even if in a symbolic way.

Hugh of Lincoln (1140–1200) was a Frenchman who came to England as a missionary and became a Carthusian bishop. He died in London and was buried in Lincoln. In 1280, while his relics were being translated, or moved, to a shrine, his head separated from the shoulder, leaving the neck fresh and red as if death had been recent. This was taken as a miracle, for the new reliquary was not long enough for both body and head. The head was placed on a silver dish to be carried through the crowd in a procession to the new shrine. Then all the relics were encased in a new coffer of gold, silver and gems, and the shrine itself was embellished with the same.

In 1364, vandals stole the head and other treasures from the shrine and abandoned the head in a field. Poor Hugh! According to lore, a raven watched over it until it was found and returned to the church. The vandals gave themselves up and were hanged.

In 1540, King Henry VIII, in his closure of churches and monasteries, ordered the shrine to be dismantled and the valuables – some 2,621 ounces of gold and 4,215 ounces of silver, plus the jewels – transported to the Tower of London. Hugh's relics were destroyed. A legend holds that somehow the relics were saved and hidden away, but no evidence exists to support the story. The only known relic remaining is a fragment of bone kept at the Grande Chartreuse in France.

The destruction of Hugh's relics – as well as the destruction of monasteries, shrines and other relics throughout England – was important symbolically as the breaking of the Catholic Church's power.

Relic Rankings

Not all relics are equal. The Church defines three classes of relics. First-class relics are actual pieces of the saint. Second-class relics are a saint's possessions and clothing, and, if a martyr, objects used in his torture and execution. Third-class relics are objects that have touched first-

and second-class relics. Miraculous healings involving relics were validated by the Vatican concerning St John Neumann (1811–60) of Philadelphia, the first American bishop and first man in America to be canonized.

John Nepomucene Neumann was born in Prachititz, Bohemia (in what is now the Czech Republic). He came to America in June 1836 and was ordained a Redemptorist priest. Active as a missionary, especially among immigrants, he established 100 churches and 80 parochial schools. He founded the School Sisters of Notre Dame. A prolific writer, he produced two popular catechisms. Pope Paul VI canonized him in 1977.

One authenticated miracle involved Eva Benassi, 11, of Sassuolo, northern Italy. She was living at boarding school in May 1923 when she was diagnosed with tubercular peritonitis. She deteriorated quickly and was prepared for death. She and others prayed for healing through the intercession of Bishop Neumann, who was credited with healing Eva's father. A picture of the bishop (a second- or third-class relic) was touched to her. During the night, she was completely healed of all symptoms.

An investigation determined that the correct diagnosis was 'acute diffused peritonitis'. The Vatican Medical College stated that her cure was instantaneous, perfect, lasting and 'naturally unexplainable'.

On the evening of 8 July 1949, music teacher J. Kent Lenahan, Jr., of Villanova, Pennsylvania, was critically injured in a car accident. He was severely crushed between a car and a telegraph pole. His injuries were so bad that he was not expected to live. His skull was crushed; a lung was badly punctured by a fractured rib; an eye was hanging out of its socket onto his cheekbone; and he was bleeding heavily from his ears, nose and mouth. His pulse was 160 and his fever rose to an incredible, life-threatening 107 degrees. He was believed to be dying.

The young man's parents obtained a piece of cassock – a second-class relic – that had belonged to bishop

Neumann and laid it on him. Miraculously, his temperature dropped to 100 degrees and his pulse to nearly normal. His injuries began to heal quickly, and he walked out of the hospital five weeks later to resume a normal life.

Miraculous Phenomena of Relics

Many relics are associated with miracles and exhibit miraculous properties. The Old Testament relates how a dead man was thrown into the grave of the prophet Elisha, and when the bones of the prophet touched the corpse, the man came back to life. In Christianity, the records kept of saints contain many accounts of miracles associated with their relics.

For example, vials of dried blood believed to be that of St Januarius liquefy several times a year. Very little is known about Januarius. He was a bishop of Benvenuto, Italy and died around 304/305. According to legend, he was beheaded during Christian persecutions.

Januarius's relics were preserved, and during the early Middle Ages his bones toured Europe. In the 14th century, his skull was enshrined in Naples. Two vials of blood, said to have been collected at his beheading, also appeared.

The first miracle of the liquefying blood was recorded in 1389, while a priest was holding the vials in a procession. Since 1659, the Church has documented the ritual liquefaction of the blood. It is kept in hermetically-sealed vials that are brought out to public display for certain occasions: the first Sunday in May, which commemorates the translation of the relics to Naples; 19 September, the feast day of the saint; and 16 December, the commemoration of the eruption of Mount Vesuvius in 1631, when the blood liquefied for 30 days. Sometimes the blood liquefies quickly, within minutes, and sometimes takes several hours to change.

More than a thousand books, articles and studies in Italian alone have been written on this miracle. Some limited scientific tests have been carried out. The Church does not allow the hermetic seals to be broken, which would ruin the blood. No natural explanation has ever been found.

The bones of a number of saints exude a strange oil or water that often has healing properties. The oil is usually odourless and tasteless, though sometimes it carries a sweet perfume. Called manna, it is collected into small vials called ampules or absorbed into cloths, and is sometimes distributed to the faithful who need healing.

The bones of St Nicholas exude manna. Nicholas, who died sometime between 345 and 352, was bishop of Myra. His generosity and gift-giving made him the model for the modern Saint Nick, or Santa Claus, of Christmas time.

In the 11th century, Nicholas's relics were translated from Myra to Bari. The bones were found to be exuding a considerable quantity of mysterious oil. It seemed to drip from the very pores of the bones. In Bari, the relics were enshrined. Numerous miracles were reported by pilgrims. The dripping manna was collected in ampules. The oil has been examined scientifically, and has been determined not to come from water or humidity.

The manna that issues from the bones of St Walburga (710–779) is called 'pearls'. Walburga was born in Devon, England. She was educated at Wimborne Monastery in Dorset, where she became a nun, and then went to Germany, where she became an abbess and spent the rest of her life. She was buried at Heidenheim. In the late ninth century, her bones were moved to Eichstadt. It was then that the relics were discovered to be secreting a clear liquid that resembled fresh water, and which had medicinal properties. It is consumed and used as an ointment. The flow begins every year between 12 October, the date her remains were moved, and stops on 25 February, the date of the anniversary of her death.

Among other saints whose bones have exuded manna are Andrew the Apostle, one of the original followers of Jesus; Teresa of Avila (1515–82), Spanish mystic and founder of the Discalced Carmelites; Gerard Majella (d. 1755), Italian Redemptorist renowned for his miraculous gifts; Elizabeth of Hungary (1207–31), a Franciscan tertiary who worked for the poor and sick; and Hugh of Lincoln, mentioned above.

PLACES

Sacred places are sites and locales where people feel they can touch the divine. They are sacred because divine beings reside there, make appearances there, or cause miraculous events to occur there. Sacred places draw millions of pilgrims who come to worship and pray in the hope of touching the divine, or for healing and miracles.

Lourdes

One of the most famous sacred sites in the world is Lourdes in southern France, a riverside grotto where the Blessed Virgin Mary made 18 appearances in 1858. Lourdes has become synonymous with miracle cures. Pilgrims come to bathe in and drink the water that comes forth from a spring. Thousands of miracle cures are claimed by individuals every year. The Church investigates some of them, and has authenticated 65. This conservative attitude does not deter millions of hopefuls from seeking their own private miracles.

Lourdes is in a region renowned for curative waters, but was itself of no particular renown prior to 1858. On 11 February that year, 14-year-old Bernadette Soubirous went out with two friends to gather firewood along the Gave du Pau river. They waded in the water near a natural grotto at a place called Massabieille. The water was cold and Bernadette, afraid of getting an asthma attack, fell behind her friends. Suddenly she heard the sound of rushing wind and saw a brilliant light near the grotto. A small woman appeared in the light and bowed her head in greeting. Bernadette got out her rosary, and the apparition prayed with her. Speaking Bernadette's dialect, the woman instructed her to come back to the grotto every day for 15 days. She said, 'I do not promise to make you happy in this world but in the next.'

Bernadette told others of her experience. Crowds came to the grotto and watched Bernadette experience 18 visions through to 4 March. Mary gave her personal messages and messages for the world in which she urged people to pray and do penitence. During the visions, Bernadette experienced trances or ecstasies, some lasting an hour.

On 25 February, Mary told Bernadette to drink from a spring, pointing to a spot on the ground. Bernadette dug into the earth, and appeared to spectators to be eating mud. A spring emerged. In the last apparition on 4

March, the woman identified herself as 'the Immaculate Conception'. One of Mary's instructions was that a church should be built on the spot where she appeared. One was soon erected.

As soon as word of the apparitions spread, pilgrims were attracted to the site. Though Mary had said nothing about healing, the pilgrims instinctively bathed in and drank the spring waters in hope of cures through her patronage and intercession. Unlike some other springs in the region, the water at Lourdes was determined to have no known natural therapeutic properties. Instead, healing came through faith and belief.

The waters seemed particularly beneficial to children who suffered from developmental problems, and to adults who suffered from crippling illness. Nonetheless, all manner of afflictions were healed. The crippled walked, the blind saw; warts, tumours and ulcers vanished. Some people collected the water to take as medicine upon their return home. Other miracles took place, too – miracles of conversion, faith and devotion, and emotional healing.

The waters were not the only medium for healing. It quickly became apparent that pilgrims were also healed in the presence of the Eucharist, especially by being touched by the monstrance containing it.

In her book *Lourdes*, Ruth Harris, a Fellow and Tutor in modern history at New College, Oxford, examines the complex social and psychological factors underlying the Lourdes phenomenon. Pilgrims automatically equated the presence of Mary with healing, as part of a grand divine scheme. 'They frequently did not see their transformations just in terms of their own cure, but as part of the Virgin's plan for mankind, a belief that echoed the way Christ's miracles were interpreted through the Gospels,' said Harris. This sense of participation in a cosmic plan certainly encourages faith and belief, two very important factors in miracles, as we shall see in the next chapter.

In 1860, a commission was established to evaluate reports of miracle cures. Many of the early reports lack medical diagnosis documentation and follow-up status reports. More formal investigation procedures were in place by the end of the 19th century.

Mary has been reported in thousands of sightings, but the Church has declared only a handful of them – six – to be authentic. Lourdes is among them. The Church authenticated Bernadette's apparitions in 1862, and canonized Bernadette as a saint on 8 December 1933. Meanwhile, Lourdes continues to attract people who seek a miracle, and miracles continue to happen.

Medjugorje

The newest major site of Marian apparitions is Medjugorje, formerly in Yugoslavia and now part of Bosnia. Like Lourdes, Medjugorje draws millions of pilgrims, many who come to ask for miracles. The site has been active since 1981, with continuing daily appearances by Mary, not just to the original visionaries, but to others as well. The Medjugorje apparitions have not yet been authenticated by the Church. Investigations are underway.

The apparitions began on 24 June 1981, when six children on a hill known as Mount Prodbro (later known as Apparition Hill) beheld a beautiful young woman holding a child and beckoning to them. She was surrounded by beautiful, brilliant rays of light. Four of the children plus two others returned to the spot the next day and saw the woman, who did not have the child. The sightings continued daily, but not always in the same place, and to others. Mary's appearance was often preceded by brilliant flashes of light. On 2 August 1981, the sun was seen to spin in the sky, similar to the spinning sun miracle at the authenticated apparitions at Fatima, Portugal, in 1917. A white cloud descended over the mountainside. Some people had visions of a great

number of angels with trumpets coming out of the sun; others saw a vision of a large heart with six small hearts.

The apparitions immediately attracted huge crowds of spectators and pilgrims. People reported miraculous phenomena, such as rosaries of plain metal turning to silver and gold, and numerous miracle cures. Since 1981, Mary has given out more than 300 messages to the public. Her main themes are peace, conversion, prayer, devotion, faith and fasting.

Medjugorje and Lourdes are but two of many sites around the world where miraculous events, phenomena and cures have been credited to appearances of Mary.

St Joseph's Oratory

An estimated two million people visit Montreal every year for the express purpose of making a pilgrimage to St Joseph's Oratory, the world's largest shrine to the father of Jesus. Most of them come in hope of a healing;

the founder of the oratory, Brother André, was a miracle healer.

Brother André was born Alfred Bessett in 1845 in a village east of Montreal. He was frail from his first breath – in fact, he was baptized immediately after birth out of fear that he would not live. He grew up small, slight and of delicate constitution. Throughout his life, his health was poor, yet the power of God flowed through him to heal others.

In 1870, he devoted himself to a life of religious service with the Congregation of the Holy Cross, a religious order dedicated to the teaching profession. He was given the name André in honour of his sponsor, Pastor André Provençal.

Unschooled and untrained, the only thing Brother André could do was pray. He was given a lowly job as doorkeeper at Notre Dame College in Mount Royal. At night he would go out and visit the sick. And they were healed. The crippled walked and the cancerous were

cured. Sometimes he rubbed holy oil on them, sometimes he touched them, sometimes he told them, like
Jesus, simply that they were healed. Like Jesus, the grace
poured out of him. He became renowned as the 'Wonder
Man of Mount Royal'. People travelled great distances to
seek his healing. He credited all his work to his patron
saint, Joseph, intercessor to the power of God.

Since Brother André lived in modern times, there are
many well-documented stories of his miraculous healing
work. One case concerned a man named Robert Moses,
who became seriously ill with peritonitis. He fell uncon-
scious for three days, and his doctor predicted that he
would not survive the next night. Robert's landlord went
out and fetched brother André and brought him to the
sick man's side. Later Robert recounted:

*The first time I regained consciousness was when Brother
André took my hand and shook it three times. He asked,
'How do you feel?' I answered with a groan. He squeezed*

my hand a second time and said, 'Something wrong?' I said, 'I feel terrible.' A third time he took my hand and shook it, and he said, 'Now it's going to be better.'

At that moment I felt relieved, as though a weight had been lifted from my brain, and down my body, and off my feet. I asked Brother André, 'Shall I be able to sleep?' He said, 'Yes, you will sleep, and tomorrow morning you'll come to the Oratory.' Then I asked, 'Shall I be able to go to the Oratory?' He said, 'If you're not sick, then there will be nothing to prevent you from coming.'

Brother André then left. Robert's temperature was taken. It had dropped to normal. The doctor told his pregnant wife this was a sign that he was about to die. Instead, Robert simply fell into a peaceful sleep. The next morning he awoke feeling well. He dressed and went to the Oratory, where he climbed the steep stairs without tiring. Brother André instructed him to get a medal of St Joseph, and to go to the altar and give thanks to the saint, which he did.

In the evening, the doctor came and found him quite recovered. The doctor said, 'I can only cure with medication, whereas Brother André can perform miracles!'

Not all of Brother André's miracles were of physical healing. One father of a family was badly in debt and was about to lose his home in foreclosure. One winter evening, Brother André was at the home of one of his supporters, Azarius Claude, who knew the man in debt but was not able to help him. The doorbell rang. A strange man stood on the step, holding a thick envelope. The man said, 'This is for Mr So-and-So,' naming the man in debt. He turned and walked off. Inside was exactly enough money to cover the debt. Brother André and Azarius dashed outside to see who the man was. But the man had vanished, and falling snow had obscured his footsteps. Brother André's conclusion: 'It must have been St Joseph.'

During his life, Brother André endured the scepticism and downright opposition of some of his peers and superiors, who doubted that such a simple man could possess so wondrous a gift. He shrugged off the poor treatment. He always worked within his religious system, gaining permission for everything he did. He prayed ceaselessly.

Brother André was by no means a perfect or faultless man. He could be brusque and gruff with people, sometimes bluntly informing them that they could not be healed because they lacked faith in the power of God or were living in sin. One man who suffered from severe stomach problems would not be healed, Brother André told him, until he stopped an adulterous affair.

The building of the oratory in honour of St Joseph was the realization of Brother André's lifelong dream. He saved small change, and enlisted the support of others. In 1904, a tiny chapel was erected on Mount Royal on grounds opposite the college. It was often filled to overflowing by those who wished to be close to Brother André. Over the years, donations funded expansions, including the huge basilica, which rises taller than any building in Montreal and holds 3,000 people.

In his later years, Brother André travelled around Canada and even to the United States, visiting New England, New York and New Jersey. He inspired Americans to make pilgrimages to Mount Royal.

He died on 3 January 1937, and was beatified in 1987 by Pope John Paul II. However, death did not end his healing power. As millions of pilgrims attest, he heals from beyond the grave.

Brother André is buried inside the oratory. His heart is on view as a relic, encased in a clear glass container. An entire wall inside the oratory is covered with canes and crutches that were discarded on the spot by people whom Brother André healed. But the real attraction, the real power centre, is his small black granite tomb, called the Black Coffin. Pilgrims come to touch the tomb and pray for healing. The touch connects them to the saint and thus through intercession to the healing power of God.

The Bishop's Shrine

St John Neumann's shrine plays a role in a miraculous healing authenticated by the Vatican for his cause for canonization.

Six-year-old Michael Flanigan of West Philadelphia suffered from osteomyelitis, an inflammation of the bones. In July 1963, while undergoing medical treatment, he was discovered to have Ewing's Sarcoma, a bone cancer that is nearly always fatal once it has spread to other sites in the body. By the time his cancer was discovered, Michael was infected in his right tibia, jaw and lungs. He was given six months to live.

His parents took him to John Neumann's shrine in Philadelphia. After several visits, he improved significantly. By Christmas 1963, all symptoms had disappeared. His healing was declared by the Vatican to be 'scientifically and medically unexplainable'.

HOLY OBJECTS

In Chapter Two, I mentioned the statues of St Jude that helped to sell homes when buried in the gardens. Does a statue of a saint hold a miraculous power of its own?

Holy statues, medals, oils and other objects do not have power themselves, but have connections to power – if we so believe. Using them, holding them and keeping them encourages a change in consciousness – we become more receptive to the possibility of something miraculous taking place. They are tools of the miraculous but we certainly have the ability to connect to the power of miracles without such tools. As Brother André knew so keenly, however, we love to have something tangible. It makes the power feel real and available.

Brother André healed many people by instructing them to rub themselves with a medal of St Joseph and St Joseph's oil. His favourite medal was a large one depicting St Joseph with the child Jesus on one side, and St

Joseph's Oratory on the other side. Some people accused him of fostering superstition and magic, but Brother André insisted the medal was a sign of faith and an expression of confidence in God. Perhaps he was just a shrewd psychologist, for he knew how much people like keepsakes and souvenirs. He gave away many medals to those he visited and treated. Undoubtedly, the medals did help to strengthen belief in a higher power. 'The oil and the medal help us think of St Joseph,' he said. 'They support our confidence in him.'

The use of holy oil has precedence in the Bible. When the Apostles went out to heal and evangelize, they anointed people with oil in the name of the Lord. Brother André distributed holy oil blessed in the Oratory. One recipient was a young man who suffered from terrible eczema; doctors had said there was nothing they could do. The young man was told to rub himself with St Joseph's oil. He did so and went to bed, and when he awoke in the morning the eczema was gone – and never returned.

Another recipient was a two-year-old boy who had deformed feet and badly twisted crippled legs. Every day since his birth, his parents had prayed for healing. None came until they met Brother André, and rubbed the boy's legs and feet with holy oil. He was healed well enough to walk.

Power in a Legend

Many people wear or carry medals of St Christopher, the patron saint of travellers. Very little is known about St Christopher; it is likely that he is mostly a legend built on a small amount of historical fact. According to legend, he was a ferryman who carried a child across a river. The child turned out to be Jesus. Despite the fact that Christopher is mostly legend, people still pray to him and consider him a protector saint.

Elaine has worn a St Christopher's medal since childhood. It has been her automatic custom to make a quick prayer for protection whenever she takes a trip. One night in a strange town, she lost her way and suddenly found herself driving in a neighbourhood that was obviously dangerous. Instinctively, she touched the medallion hanging around her neck and whispered a prayer of protection.

When she stopped at a stop sign, two men suddenly appeared out of nowhere. One pointed a large gun at her through the window. 'Get out of the car, now!' he shouted. Instantly, several dreadful scenarios ran through her mind: carjacking, kidnapping, rape, murder. But Elaine did not scream or panic. Instead, with the utmost calm, she rolled down her window and gave the assailants a dazzling smile. 'Can I give you boys a lift somewhere?' she said. For a heart-stopping moment, nothing happened. Then the man with the gun waved her away. 'Go on, get out of here,' he snapped. Elaine wasted no time speeding away. She drove blindly for a few minutes and then stopped. Shock set in, and she shook violently.

Later, Elaine struggled to understand what had happened. A presence had somehow come over her. How could she otherwise explain her bizarre behaviour and total calmness? A key was her saint's medallion – it made her feel connected to the protection of God. 'I prayed for protection,' she said. 'Only a miracle prevented something disastrous from happening.'

A sceptic would scoff at the idea that a legendary saint whose life was probably mostly fiction could intervene. But the factual life of a saint is not as important as the belief and faith in the power of God that the saint generates in the living.

CHAPTER FIVE

MIRACLES IN
DAILY LIFE

 We experience the miraculous in many ways. The miracles of everyday life can take the form of dramatic ones such as those of the saints, or they can be personal miracles that have meaning just for us.

Actually, there is no difference between 'big' miracles and 'little' miracles in terms of importance. All miracles are important, whether they save our lives or shift our attitudes towards life.

Here are other avenues through which miracles come.

SYNCHRONICITY

Sometimes a synchronicity is a miracle: we find ourselves in the right place at the right time for something deeply meaningful and transformative to happen.

Aspiring entrepreneur Louis P. found himself in a desperate financial situation. He had started his own business, but unexpected expenses, legal issues and a family health crisis had drained his resources dangerously low. He was like an aeroplane struggling to lift off, certain everything was going to crash.

Louis piled up debt until he had nowhere to turn, and no money on which to keep going. Filing for bankruptcy seemed to be the only option. He felt humiliated at the prospect. But what hurt even more was the prospect of admitting failure with his business. There were friends and family members who would stand in line to say, 'I told you so'.

One day, Louis was walking along the street and passed a rubbish bin. It was full, and something on top caught his eye. It was a small book that looked brand new, like it had never been opened. It was resting on top of the refuse as though someone had carefully laid it there. The book was about how to manifest prosperity. Normally Louis would never pluck anything out of a bin, but the book seemed pristine. It seemed to beckon to him. Curious, he took it. Later that night, he read it. The book was full of optimistic advice. Louis was uplifted and heartened. He thought, 'Maybe it's not too late for anything to help.'

A few days later, Louis received a phone call. He was told he was going to receive some money from a completely unexpected source. It wasn't enough to solve his entire financial dilemma, but it would enable him to avoid filing for bankruptcy. He would have breathing space, and a chance to recover. 'I honestly believe that my receiving the money just when I did was nothing short of a miracle,' he said. 'It had to be.' As for the book, that too was a miracle. 'I now have a plan of spiritual principles for changing my consciousness for the better,' he said.

If we measure what happened to Louis by religious standards, it would not be called a miracle. But shouldn't 'miracle' be a matter of personal perspective? Louis's life was changed in an unforeseen, unexpected and unexplained way. He definitely saw the hand of God in the way events unfolded. A divine orchestration was necessary to bring Louis and the book together. Then a financial 'angel' appeared, just at the right time to avoid a disastrous turn of events. Perhaps most important was his change in consciousness – an uplifting that enabled him to envision possibilities, even if nothing tangible was directly in front of him.

'This may sound strange, but now I feel that there really is a God,' Louis said. 'Don't get me wrong – I've always believed in God. But God seemed rather remote. I thought miracles were things that happened only in the Bible and to special people. What happened to me made me feel that I am very much a part of God's plan, and I have a faith that I didn't have before.'

SIGNS

Sometimes a sign is a miracle: we get a mysterious signal from God that we are on the right track, or that all is well and in divine order.

American artist and writer Carol R. Resch lost her niece, Ann, to thyroid cancer. The two were close, and Ann even bore a strong resemblance to Carol. The presence of angels was prominent in their lives. Carol drew them and wrote about them, and felt their loving presence. Ann felt this presence, too. As her illness progressed, the presence became stronger and stronger. As she lay in her hospital bed, her body weakened from disease, she could feel their immense wings enfolding her in comfort, and hear their rustlings.

Finally the cancer became too much, and Ann passed away. About 200 people attended her funeral service, including Carol, her husband, Larry, and their longtime friend, Nellie, who had been a nurse. The casket was open for viewing, and friends and family filed past to pay their last loving respects.

From where she sat on the pew, Carol could see Ann's face. She was gazing at it as a relative sat down in front of her in her line of sight. As he sat, a ray of light came through the overhead skylight of the church. The beam came between Carol's vision, the man and Ann's face. In an instant, Carol felt Ann's spirit lifted up to heaven by angels.

A white feather fell mysteriously from the ceiling of the church right into Ann's casket. Her face radiated peace and contentment. Carol saw the feather. Larry saw it. Nellie saw it. It was a sign to Carol that angels do exist, and they had come to take Ann home. The miraculous feather reaffirmed the presence and love of God, and divine order.

HANDS OF GOD

Many miracles involve a palpable, invisible presence that pushes us or takes hold of us. The 'hands of God' often manifest in an emergency. With them come an intuitive feeling that we are being saved or guided by God, an angel, a divine being, or even a watchful loved one who has passed to the Other Side. In Chapter One, we saw an example of the 'hands of God' – the push that moved little Jess out of the way of an oncoming car.

Dolores Warner's father, grandmother and uncle all died within a period of about two months. They had all lived about 150 miles away, in New Jersey. The morning her father died of cancer, Dolores felt his presence in her bedroom. She awakened to a circle of light and energy flying around the room. The telephone was ringing. She knew immediately her father had passed, and he was saying goodbye. The call confirmed her feelings – her mother was on the line with the difficult news that Dad had passed away. When her uncle died soon afterwards, Dolores experienced the same thing.

Dolores attended the funeral with her daughter, Alyson. It was an emotionally draining, difficult day. Finally, they left for the long drive back home. First, they stopped at the cemetery where her father was buried, and spent some time at his grave. From there, they headed for the motorway.

Dolores and Alyson talked about the day as Dolores turned the car onto the long sliproad. As she accelerated, she noticed roadworks on the road ahead of her that blocked the shoulder of the road on the right. Suddenly, Dolores felt a hand take hold of her right shoulder. The grip was strong and warm. She turned to look, but no one was in the back seat. What she did see terrified her. Roaring down the road behind her at high speed was a lorry. 'Oh, my God!' she gasped. For a split second, she thought they would crash into the roadworks. Instinctively, she pulled the car left and was able to enter the other lane. The truck sped past. 'Did you see that?' she exclaimed to Alyson. Dolores was so shaken by the near-miss that she had to pull over to the side of the road and compose herself.

'It was so amazing that I was still alive,' she said later. 'Whatever it was that made me turn my head saved my life. I felt that it was my Dad. I was really close to him, and think of him as a guardian angel.' The experience made both Dolores and Alyson more aware of extraordinary events, and the intervention of the miraculous in life.

Juli, whom we met in Chapter One, also had an experience with the 'hands of God'.

One day Juli discovered she had locked herself out of her house. She knew the sliding glass door on the back balcony was unlocked – but the balcony was on the first floor. Juli looked at the fence around the small back yard and saw that if she climbed it, she would be able to reach out and grab the wooden railing around the balcony.

The climb was tricky and Juli struggled for balance. She was able to get one foot planted on the side of the balcony, and she grabbed two of the slats in the railing. To her shock, they gave way and came off in her hands. She felt herself careening backwards and could not stop her fall. Then, amazingly, before she struck ground, she felt a pressure beneath her, moving her back up. Someone, or something, invisible pushed her upright and up over the balcony railing. She touched down on the balcony light as a feather.

Was it the hands of God, or a guardian angel, or her deceased mother? Juli was certain only that 'someone up above' was watching out for her.

A MIRACLE OF HEALING

Yvette is a spiritual teacher of self-healing who lives in Lincoln, England, a fascinating northern city where Roman ruins coexist with the medieval and the modern. The centrepiece of Lincoln is its great cathedral, built atop the city's highest point, and once the tallest structure in Europe. At night, when the cathedral glows in lights, it seems a focal point for the meeting of heaven and earth – a fitting backdrop for a miracle of healing.

A tumour on her pituitary gland changed Yvette's life and put her in touch with miracles. The tumour was not malignant, but it seriously affected her health. Her immune system was depressed. She had severe anaemia and impaired eyesight. She suffered from frequent headaches and 'pins and needles' in her arms. Her hormones were out of balance. She was told she probably would never be able to have children, and if she became pregnant she might not survive. Married but childless at the time, Yvette very much wanted to have a family, a normal life. She knew nothing about healing then, and never thought of herself as having any remarkable abilities.

But life was anything but normal. The marriage was stormy and she struggled with many severe health problems associated with the tumour. Somehow Yvette managed to conceive and safely bear two children, a son and a daughter. The marriage broke up.

A turning point came when Yvette suddenly found herself 'open'. It seemed to be the result of all the misery and trauma she had experienced. She was now sensitive in ways she had not been before. She could sense the energy fields around others and 'know' things about them. She began to exhibit an ability to heal with her hands. In shamanism, an initiate must heal himself to earn his title. Yvette did not yet realize it, but a self-healing challenge lay before her.

Yvette remarried and thought about having more children. Life became happy instead of turbulent. However, the tumour continued to wreak havoc with her body and health. She had episodes of fainting. She was advised to have the tumour removed by surgery before complications worsened – although her odds of recovering from the surgery were given at 50:50.

For 11 years, the tumour had drastically affected her life. Now she was at a crisis point – the tumour had to go. Yvette had a deep knowing within her that surgery was not the answer. In fact, she was certain that if she had the surgery, she would die. The only way she would be rid of the tumour would be to heal herself. It would be a miracle if she did. How could she accomplish it?

Yvette was allergic to pineapple. So severe was her allergy that eating the fruit required a rush to hospital.

One day a thought arose in her mind: 'If I can cure myself of an allergy to pineapple, then surely I can cure the tumour. I have to believe, truly, in every inch of me, that I won't have an allergy to pineapple.'

Yvette prepared herself by establishing and reinforcing her belief that she had no allergy to pineapple. When she felt ready to test herself, she instructed her husband, Peter, to go out and buy her a meal in which pineapple was an ingredient, though not an obvious one. She ate it and then told Peter what she had done. Panicked, he asked, 'Shouldn't we go to hospital right now?' She assured him she would be fine.

Yvette had no reaction. Not even a small one. She realized, with a certainty of her entire being, that she now could heal herself of the tumour, too. The pineapple allergy had seemed manageable. The tumour had loomed as a giant task. The pineapple test brought the tumour down to size.

The healing began spontaneously during meditation one day. An image of a river arose in Yvette's mind:

I walked along the riverbank and sat down. There was a pile of rubble in the river that blocked the water flow. I knew I had to clear it. I started to lift the stones and throw them into the river. The rubble was my tumour.

A few days later, while I was meditating, the image of the river came again. There was still rubble in the middle. I again lifted out large black stones and threw them into the river.

The river came again a third time in meditation. This time I was surprised to see that the rubble had exploded all over. Then I saw a large man approach me, very dark and tall. He came up from behind and wrapped himself around me. He asked me what I wanted to do with the tumour. I realized that he was a spirit of cancer. I told him that I wanted to hand it back now.

He said, 'Are you sure?'

I said, 'Yes, I don't want it anymore.' I handed it to him.
When I looked at the rubble I realized that I had come to
an acceptance within myself that I didn't need the illness
anymore. Maybe part of me had accepted it and wanted
it because I had had such a miserable life.

But the miracle was not completely finished. 'I knew I
had to repair all the damages caused by the tumour, one
by one,' said Yvette. 'I worked on them one at a time in
meditation, and saw them being healed. It took about
four years to repair all the damage.' Yvette was able to
have two more children, another daughter and another
son. 'I always knew I was meant to have four children,'
she said.

Similar cases of miraculous, self-directed healing
have been documented in medical journals, especially
concerning people who have catastrophic illness.
Visualizations, meditation, prayer and divine intercession from angels and saints often are given by patients

as being responsible. The medical profession categorizes such cases under 'spontaneous remission', meaning that no known reasons for the cures exist.

Somehow these people are able to access divine currents of power that enable miraculous healing. The power moulds itself to the needs of each case: here it manifests as a saint, there it manifests as a divine being coming in a dream, and elsewhere it manifests with appropriate imagery in a meditation.

Yvette followed her intuition in determining what to do. 'I never prayed to remove the tumour. It needed more than prayer. Something deep inside me had to want it to go. Every inch of me had to not want it.

'I learned a lot about myself,' she continued. 'I felt that I had encouraged the tumour and illnesses. I had been pushed around all my life and suddenly I wasn't having any of it. I completely transformed from being weak to being strong. I learned to love myself – that's the biggest miracle.

'People don't fully understand the power of visualization,' said Yvette. 'It's hard to get across to people that our minds are so strong. It's amazing what we can do to ourselves, and what we can make ourselves do. People can't see it or feel it, but the power is there. You determine whether it will work for you or against you.

'We have the power to make miracles happen. They are not just God's thing. We are all part of God. He doesn't keep the power for himself to dish out – it's there for all to see and to use. God gave us the ability to have miracles, but we don't use it.

'A miracle is in the eye of the beholder. Anything can be a miracle, but the biggest miracle is awakening to ourselves. The first and most important step is to truly understand that we all have the power. Then we can believe. And we can make miracles happen for others.'

As part of her healing, Yvette strives to help others wake up to themselves and become empowered.

Let's turn now to what science can tell us about miracles.

CHAPTER SIX

PSI, SCIENCE AND METAPHYSICS

 The same phenomena in miracles, miraculous powers and the siddhi and iddhi are studied in parapsychology as paranormal phenomena.

'Psi' involves extra-sensory perception and psycho-kinesis. Extra-sensory perception, or ESP, includes telepathy, clairvoyance, clairaudience and clairsentience (the ability to experience things beyond the senses). Psychokinesis, or PK, is the influence of mind over matter: the manipulation of the physical world with consciousness, or one's thought, intent and will. 'Macro PK', or PK on a large scale, includes mental movement and influence of objects, materializations, levitation, bilocation, teleportation, multiplication, and the production of objects seemingly out of thin air, or 'apports'. 'Micro PK' involves influence over matter on atomic and subatomic levels. In a nutshell, psi is 'our experience of the invisible connections that bind the universe together', in the words of American parapsychologist Dean Radin.

In the terms of psychical research, or parapsychology as it is known today, the objects produced by saints such as Sai Baba are apports. The picture of Jesus which Juli's deceased mother gave her (*see page 12*) is also an apport: an object sent from the spiritual realm into the physical realm.

For well over a century, science has attempted to study and measure psi, but very little has been scientifically proven because phenomena are hard to measure and even harder to create on demand for a laboratory experiment. Rather, science has collected a lot of 'evidence in support of' psi. So much evidence has been accumulated that psi is acknowledged to exist, though we still know little about how and why it functions. Parapsychology attempts to understand this by studying the interactions between consciousness and the physical world. What we have discovered about psi has implications not only for miracles, but for our whole approach to humanity.

Early Research

From the 19th century to the 1930s, most psychical research focused on mediums and mediumship.

Mediums have been known by various names, among them oracle, soothsayer, wizard, cunning woman, wise woman, fortune teller, witch, witch doctor, medicine man, sorcerer, shaman, mystic, priest, prophet and chanteller. However, distinctions are often made between these terms. According to anthropologist Michael Winkelman, the role of the medium – and of several other magico-religious practitioner types – developed historically out of that of the shaman.

There are two types of mediumship: mental and physical. In mental mediumship, the medium communicates with the spirit realm through means such as inner vision, clairaudience, automatic writing and automatic speech. Physical mediumship is characterized by rappings; table-tipping; levitation of objects or the medium; movement of objects; materializations of spirits and objects (apports); and the production of ghostly music, 'spirit lights' and strange scents. The principle of physical mediumship is that it is accomplished in a partnership with spirits – who use the medium as a vehicle.

The origins of modern mediumship began in research on mesmerism during the 19th century. Some subjects who were 'magnetized', or hypnotized, into trances fell under the control of spirits and delivered messages from the Other Side. Like shamans who communicate with the spirit world by becoming possessed by godlings, spirit animals and deities, the mesmeric subjects became temporarily 'possessed' by discarnate spirits.

Also in the 19th century, spiritualism exploded on both sides of the Atlantic, and physical mediumship was central to it. After the turn of the 20th century, the First World War brought tens of thousands of bereaved to seance tables. People attended in the hope that a medium could produce phenomena believed to come from the spirit world, especially signs or messages from dead loved ones. Some fraud was exposed – but many of the witnessed phenomena went unexplained by science.

Agnes Guppy was the first medium to perform full-form spirit materializations in England, and reigned as queen of spiritualist circles from the mid-1860s to the early 1870s. She was especially famous for her spectacular apports, including fresh flowers, fruit, sand and ice. In June 1871, she was allegedly teleported to a seance at a home in High Holborn, London, dressed in only her robe and holding her pen and household account book. One of the sitters at the seance had jokingly asked the spirits present – known as John King and Katie King – if they could bring Guppy, a very large woman, and they obliged.

Physical mediumship declined in popularity as public interest waned, and researchers turned to other avenues of exploring paranormal phenomena. But in the late 1990s, a case was made public in England that renewed the debate and controversy concerning physical mediumship.

From 1994 to 1998, a group known as the Scole Experimental Group conducted physical mediumship seances in Scole, Norfolk. The Scole group said they worked with a team of spirits for the purpose of creating a new energy for 'transdimensional communication'.

The group produced at least 43 different types of phenomena, among them apports, materializations of walking forms, direct voices, levitations, raps, luminous pillars of light and ringing bells. The most striking phenomenon of all the sittings was light activity. For example, a single light would dart around the darkened cellar at great speed, even entering a crystal to light it from within. It would change shape, activate Ping-Pong balls, make sharp sounds when it hit the table, and irradiate and levitate crystals and Perspex bowls. Photographic images appeared on blank rolls of film that had been locked in boxes.

Some of the group's sittings were attended and investigated by prominent psychical researchers, including some members of the Society for Psychical Research. While investigators found no evidence of fraud, opinions on the authenticity of the phenomena were sharply divided in the parapsychological community.

INDIVIDUAL ABILITIES

The 1930s ushered in an era of controlled laboratory experiments that were evaluated statistically. Test subjects were not celebrity mediums, but average people, mostly student volunteers. Their own abilities were tested – spirits were not part of the equation. One of the premier centres for this type of research was in the United States – the J.B. Rhine laboratory at Duke University in Durham, North Carolina.

Experiments involved forced-choice tests, such as guessing cards in telepathy and clairvoyance tests, and results were evaluated statistically against chance. PK experiments involved such things as mentally affecting plant growth, moving small objects, affecting the casting of dice, changing room temperatures and the properties of water, and affecting the selection of numbers in random number generator machines.

Many of these experiments were conducted at a distance – that is, the test subject influenced something in another location, often very far away. They demonstrated quite dramatically that consciousness is not confined in the brain or mind but is non-local and can act on things not present. For example, American healer Olga Worrall prayed for rye grass seedlings 600 miles away and significantly influenced their rate of growth.

PROCESS OF PSI

By the 1960s, research interest turned to the psychological processes involved in psi. Experiments became 'process-oriented', that is, on how psi performance is affected by variables such as altered states of consciousness, time, distance, mood, personality and attitude towards psi. Tests were devised for free-response ESP (instead of forced-choice). Here subjects described whatever images or information came to mind. Researchers found a 'sheep and goat effect': people who believed in psi were more likely to test well for it, and people who did not believe in psi were more likely to test poorly. Other significant free-response research was in remote viewing, the seeing of distant objects clairvoyantly or by out-of-body travel.

Sufficient tests have been done to show that people can perform and experience psi, often at will, though with unpredictable results. But what enables them to do it? Is it strictly an inner power, or something in human consciousness that interacts with forces on a higher level? Psychically sensitive people feel a connection to something spiritual, even if they do not define it according to traditional religious ideas. So the mysterious ingredient or power we associate with miracles is definitely beyond or transcendent – but it also lies within us.

FIELD CONSCIOUSNESS

One of the more recent developments in parapsychology is research of field consciousness, an integrative view of the universe. Field consciousness addresses the underlying unity of all things: fields held together and unbounded by space and time. These fields have the ability to organize matter on a large scale – a collective PK. 'Global consciousness' and 'group mind' are other ways of describing aspects of field consciousness. In a nutshell, field consciousness places the paranormal powers experienced by the individual into the context of the whole.

Field consciousness is not a new idea by any means. The concept of an underlying unity of all things is part of our most ancient mystical philosophies. In quantum mechanics, the universe is held together by fields of probabilities that do not exist in space and time, but keep all things interconnected in such a way that a change in one place instantly affects another place without any exchange of energy.

Field consciousness may explain why some miracles happen. We are in the right place at the right time. We have a need, and the field consciousness around us helps to catalyse the experience. The group mind functions as saint or yogi.

The Maharishi Mahesh Yogi, the founder of Transcendental Meditation, was among the first to demonstrate to a modern audience how group consciousness can exert PK to affect daily life. In the 1980s, his people tested his hypothesis that if a sufficient number of people did TM at the same time, group consciousness would be raised to a higher level and there would be a decrease in crime, accidents, medical emergencies, armed conflict and other problems. TM researchers say they have replicated results affirming this hypothesis in at least 42 studies. Sociologists, however, criticize the results, saying that variables are too difficult to control.

Nonetheless, the idea has been tested successfully in more controlled laboratory settings. Parapsychologist Dean Radin has overseen experiments in which fluctuations in a group's attention were measured simultaneously against the behaviour of one or more physical systems. For example, huge audiences who had tuned in to global television broadcasts, such as the Olympic Games, were measured against random number generators. A high group coherence corresponded to a high ordering of numbers, demonstrating that group mind does affect matter. Similar tests by others have replicated these results.

One interesting study examined the effect of group consciousness on weather. Most of us think we have no control over weather, but in shamanism it is accepted, even required, that a shaman know how to influence the elements. The study suggests that mind influence of weather exists all the time: if sufficient numbers of people expect a certain kind of weather, it is likely to happen.

The study examined a long-standing popular belief at Princeton University in New Jersey which stated that the weather would always be good for graduation exercises. An examination of 30 years' worth of weather for Princeton and surrounding communities showed that weather is unusually good at graduation time, by odds of 20 to 1.

Radin comments, 'As the mind moves, so moves matter.'

A NEW WORLD VIEW

These and other studies have significant ramifications for the responsibility of thought. We see and receive what we expect. Individual thoughts collect in pools and take on momentum.

The PK effects of group mind have significant ramifications for the order of the world. Says Radin:

These studies ... suggest that a previously unsuspected cause of global violence and aggression may literally be the chaotic, malevolent thoughts of large numbers of people around the world. For example, the idea of a jihad, a holy war against infidels, which is fervently maintained by millions throughout the world, may not only directly (e.g. through terrorist acts) but also indirectly disrupt the social order around the world. By contrast, peaceful protests such as those embodied by Gandhi and Martin Luther King, which fostered noble intentions among groups, may have been successful not only for psychological reasons, but also for physical reasons that we are only now beginning to glimpse.

Such ideas have been expressed in religious and philosophical perspectives, but their presence in science demands our attention even more, for science has been our dominant medium for explaining the nature of all things for several hundred years. Classical science has denied the importance of consciousness, but a bold new science is in the making. Social order and world events are not the only things that need re-examining from the perspective of consciousness. Things that have been called miraculous, mystical, magical and paranormal are natural parts of the universe and are integrated with our consciousness. If we can influence the weather and cause social disruption, we can also bring peace and the miraculous into being.

Willis Harman, an American philosopher of science, observed that science should not be asking such questions as 'How can we explain PK?' but rather 'How can we understand why our minds have such a limited effect in the physical world?' Shifting our emphasis makes all the difference.

Similarly, we should not ask, 'Why do miracles happen?' but rather 'Why do we not make more miracles happen?'

The traditional religious view of the miracle-worker is that the ability comes through exceptional holiness and closeness to God – something most of us never expect to attain in our lifetime. The miracle-worker achieves this state of consciousness by choices and acts available to everyone: devotion, spiritual study and the practice of a right and moral life. In short, they have an exceptional attunement to God and to the integrated fabric of the universe. Few of us may get to the level of the saints of history; however, everything we think, say and act out does affect our individual life and also contributes to a group miracle-making consciousness.

A Group Mind Makes a Difference

Robert H. Coxon of Montreal is one of Canada's most talented musicians and composers. His music is often described as 'celestial' and 'a journey into light'. Robert doesn't just compose and play music – he *is* music.

His ability to reach profound depths has been influenced by his spiritual and metaphysical study. At a young age he was introduced to the affirming principles of New Thought through Unity. He learned Silva mind control. Both New Thought and Silva taught him how to use positive thinking and intent to bring things into manifestation. He learned how to attune himself to energy and presence. He learned how music opens consciousness and penetrates to the soul.

Coxon has a personal story about the miraculous effects of group mind consciousness. He travels with Lee Carroll, channel for the entity known as Kryon, who has a large international following. The events draw large crowds who come to hear the spiritual teachings of Kryon. Robert plays the music. These events establish a group consciousness and raise it to a high level of awareness.

After one conference in Brussels, the presenters had to travel immediately by van to Paris to set up for another event. In one van were Robert, his wife, Lina, and Lee Carroll and his publisher. Robert was driving. They were

followed by another van containing author Gregg
Braden and his wife and several others:

*They drive fast on these roads in Europe. We were doing
about 150 kilometres an hour, and still everyone else on
the road was passing us. A car passed me, going
extremely fast, and just when it got ahead of me, the driver seemed to fall asleep. He veered off to the left and hit
the guard rail on the central reservation. His car started
spinning around fast and parts started flying off the car
– the bonnet, mirrors, everything. I didn't know if he was
going to spin into us or flip over. Nothing hit us. We
stopped as soon as we could and raced to the other car,
which had come to a stop. Incredibly, the driver was all
right. I was in shock. We went up to a service station off
the road and said a prayer.*

*It was a miracle that all the stuff flying off his car
missed us. But the real miracle was that the man was
not hurt at all. His car was a total wreck. Maybe our*

level of consciousness saved this guy. We were united in consciousness.

The two parties had spent hours together focused on spiritual matters. There had been teachings and meditation. When consciousness is thus raised, we enter a zone of power and potential. This zone may have prevented serious injury to everyone involved.

Robert believes that miracles are a natural part of authentic living. When we find our path and truth and live it, our limited horizon expands to access higher realities – and the power of miracles. 'Miracles are not something strange and out of reach,' he said. 'They are part of true reality. And true reality is perfect health, infinite wisdom, total abundance, and inner peace.'

If consciousness impacts reality, then our thoughts and beliefs take on a new importance.

CHAPTER SEVEN

THE POWER OF
THOUGHT AND BELIEF

 One of the fundamental
metaphysical laws of the universe
is that thought creates reality.
What we think becomes manifest.
What we believe comes to pass.

Our thoughts form beliefs – convictions held within the deep centre of our being. Thoughts and beliefs in turn fuel our faith: faith in ourselves, in our abilities, in our connection to something higher, and in the inherent goodness of the natural order.

If we believe in something wholeheartedly, we open ourselves to the power of manifestation, to bring what we believe into being. Thought is the very foundation of manifestation, for we cannot bring things into being without first thinking them. 'Thought creates reality' is a spiritual law found in all mystical traditions. Our life and our world – the things that happen to us – spring from our thoughts and beliefs. We literally *are* what we think.

The power of thought and belief is an ancient truth, but one that has lost its prominence in Western thought. Western philosophy evolved to separate mind from body. Aristotle, one of the early principal architects of this world view, held that everything that can be known about the world must come through the senses of the body; all else is illusion. Thus, the power of thought to influence reality is denied. The paranormal – things that happen beyond the five senses and the known laws of science – also have no place in this scheme.

Not all great thinkers have subscribed to this dominant view, however. In the 19th century, for example, transcendentalism merged Western and Eastern philosophies, and the 'New Thought' movement arose. Ralph Waldo Emerson, a transcendentalist, observed that 'We become what we think about all day long.'

A prominent New Thought proponent was Ernest Holmes, the founder of Science of Mind, which has grown into a huge international movement. Science of Mind teaches that we are surrounded by an Infinite Intelligence, or Mind (God), which functions upon our beliefs. If we let go of destructive beliefs and replace them with constructive ones, we enter into a co-operation with this Mind that enables us to be healthier, happier, more successful and more spiritually fulfilled.

According to Holmes, there is but one Mind and everything is an aspect of it; each of us uses a portion of it. He taught that by controlling our thinking we can control our experiences and thus improve life. 'Mind responds to mind,' said Holmes.

Holmes taught the use of affirmations – strong, positive statements – as a way of training thought to change reality. When trouble strikes, we fall into negative thinking, which exacerbates our circumstances. Positive thinking helps to restore equilibrium and harmony. For example, if you were ill, you would use an affirmation such as 'I enjoy perfect health' as part of your consciousness regimen.

Other proponents of the power of affirmations were Charles and Myrtle Fillmore, whose non-denominational Unity School of Christianity in Kansas City, Missouri, also developed from the New Thought era. Myrtle, sickly from birth, was diagnosed with terminal tuberculosis.

Doctors told her there was nothing more they could do for her. She was inspired by a lecture to completely heal herself with a regimen of prayer and affirmations, in which she affirmed that 'I am a child of God and therefore I do not inherit sickness.' Inspired in turn by her success, Charles healed himself of a severely crippled leg and partial deafness through prayer. Charles defined an affirmation as 'a positive and orderly statement of Truth. By affirmation we claim and appropriate what is ours'. Both of them claimed their health, and it was restored.

But making positive statements is not enough to empower thought. Affirmations don't produce what we expect if they only float on the surface of the ocean of our consciousness. They must penetrate into our depths and grab hold, so that we truly believe what we are thinking with every cell in our being. Only then can true change take place.

As modern interest has grown in the paranormal, alternative healing modalities and exploration of consciousness, the Western world view about the power of thought, belief and faith is gradually being redefined.

Several decades ago in England, an amazing accidental discovery led to a breakthrough on the effects of thought. George De La Warr, a psychically-gifted civil engineer, and his wife, Marjorie, an osteopath, began experimenting with the alleged healing powers of radionics using plants. Radionics involves the radiation of energies by mechanical devices.

The De La Warrs were successful in affecting the germination and growth rates of plants with such devices. After three years of intense work, they had a shattering realization: a human factor was inextricably bound up in the results of their experiments. For instance, seedlings planted in vermiculite that assistants *believed* had been treated to enhance growth – but in fact had not – grew as if they had been in treated vermiculite.

It seemed like a miracle: human thought could influence cell formation. All one had to do to get plants to flourish was ask them to do so.

George took his discovery to one of the country's leading physicists, who scoffed at him, 'I do not believe you, Mr De La Warr. If you can affect the number of atoms in a growing plant by your thought process, we must revise our concept of what constitutes matter.'

De La Warr answered, 'Indeed we must, even if such revision poses a whole overhaul of existing knowledge. How, for instance, could this energy be incorporated into mathematical equations? What would happen to the law of the conservation of energy?'

De La Warr also encountered opposition from the Catholic Church, which told him no one below the rank of a deacon had any business trying to bless plants to get them to grow.

Although many scientists still resist the idea that consciousness has a physical effect, words like 'intentionality' have become part of the language of complementary medicine. The overhaul is in process. Results similar to those of the De La Warr experiments have also been achieved using prayer.

The influence of thought and belief have been further documented in parapsychology, not only as the sheep–goat effect concerning subjects (*see page 132*), but also the 'experimenter effect' concerning the researchers themselves. The belief of the experimenter influences the results of experiments. An experimenter sceptical of psi, for example, will get more negative results in the same tests than one who believes in psi, even if he follows proper, objective protocols.

THE PLACEBO EFFECT

If plants respond to thought, then does the human body respond to thought as well? Some of the strongest evidence in support of reality-creating thought comes from the annals of medicine. Studies of the placebo effect and of prayer have demonstrated that consciousness can and does influence events in the material world. Perception is reality.

In drug tests, placebos are administered to a control group. The participants do not know whether they are receiving the drug or a 'useless' pill. Consistently, some people who take the placebos experience results the same as or better than those taking the real medication. The obvious answer is that their *expectation* and *belief* that they might be receiving the real medication somehow activates the appropriate physical response in the body.

The placebo effect has been controversial within the medical field, and many doctors dismiss it as meaningless. However, research has demonstrated how the body's complex system of chemicals and hormones responds to our thoughts and feelings. 'We don't yet understand all the ways in which brain chemicals are related to emotions and thoughts, but the salient point is that our state of mind has an immediate and direct effect on our state of body,' says prominent cancer surgeon Dr Bernie S.

Siegel in his book *Love, Medicine & Miracles*. 'We can change the body by dealing with how we feel.'

Doctors also know that patients are likely to experience whatever they are told, whether it be side-effects of tests and medications, a diagnosis or 'certain' death from cancer within a specified time frame. The doctor is held to be the authority, and so the patient believes what he is told. For example, a 1988 study at Brown University in the United States showed that people diagnosed with chronic pain were more likely to suffer impairment if they believed that pain implied impairment. The severity of pain made no difference; the belief did.

One of the growing number of doctors who reject the established notion that biology is separate from belief is Herbert Benson, associate professor of medicine at Harvard University and Deaconness Hospital, and a pioneer in research into the mind and body connection. 'Our brains are wired for beliefs and expectancies,' says Dr Benson in his book, *Timeless Healing: The Power and*

Biology of Belief. 'When activated, the body can respond as it would if the belief were a reality, producing deafness or thirst, health or illness.'

LIFE IS THE RESULT OF WHAT WE BELIEVE

In other arenas of life, the power of thought and belief is also at work. Athletes especially understand the importance of believing in their ability to perform and win. No one ever crossed a finish line first doubting his or her chances of winning. Similarly, those who get to the top of their art, profession or career have solid beliefs in themselves and their abilities to reach their goals.

According to Dr Wayne W. Dyer, popular psychotherapist, we can better understand the power of thought if we think of thought as being outside ourselves as well as within. 'Thought is much more than something that you do,' says Dyer in his book, *You'll See It*

When You Believe It. 'It is in fact what you, and all the rest of us, are as well ... You relate to everything and everyone on this planet through the mechanism of thought. It is not what is in the world that determines the quality of your life, it is how you choose to process your world in your thoughts.'

Thus, thought is not limited to your brain, but is part of your field of consciousness that extends out into the universe. Your field is interwoven with all other fields, including the field of God. The entire tapestry fluctuates in accordance to waves of individual and collective thoughts.

THOUGHT, BELIEF AND MIRACLES

These fundamental principles relating to thought and belief also apply to miracles. If we believe in the power of a saint's intercession, we open ourselves to the possibility of experiencing just such a thing. If we believe that angels always protect us from danger, then when danger threatens, we may have an experience that validates our belief. If we believe in miracles, we are predisposed to experiencing them. In fact, belief may be all we need for them to happen.

One of the healing stories told about Jesus in the Gospel of Mark concerns a woman who had suffered from haemorrhages for 12 years. Doctors had been unable to help her. She came up behind Jesus and touched his cloak, believing that this in itself would cure her. Immediately, her bleeding stopped and she felt healing through her body.

At the same time as the woman was feeling healed, Jesus felt power leave his body. Identifying who touched him, he told her, 'Daughter, your faith has made you well; go in peace, and be healed of your disease.'

It's useless for a sceptic to argue about whether or not saints really intercede from heaven to facilitate miracles, or whether angels really exist, or whether an object holds some sort of power. Events organize themselves around our thoughts and beliefs. The only truth which matters is the truth held by the individual. Belief makes a crucial difference.

Lourdes testimonials repeatedly underscore the intensity of belief and faith held by the cured. In the 19th century, for example, 13-year-old Henri Busquet had a recurring tumour in the glands of his neck. Doctors repeatedly drained it, but it always returned. Busquet went to Lourdes where he drank the water with 'faith and confidence'. He poured water on his dirty dressing. Several days later he was cured, verified by his doctors.

In an 1895 account, belief appears to have been crucial in order for a crippled woman to accept healing. Virginie Gordet came on her crutches to be immersed in one of the communal bathing pools that had been constructed:

On contact with the water, the sick woman said: 'Lord, may your will be done.' It seemed to her that her limbs were relaxing, that their strength was returning. But she dared not yet believe and went on repeating: 'Saint Mary, pray for me! Blessed Virgin, cure me!' The women who assisted her were moved to the depths of their souls. At their suggestion, and without any indication of difficulty or suffering, Mme Gordet took a few steps in the piscine [pool], then, alone, submerged herself a second time. 'But you are cured!' exclaimed the ladies. 'Ah! Help me, mesdames, to thank the Blessed Virgin.'

Gordet then stepped out of the pool on her own and prostrated herself before a statue of Mary and recited the *Magnificat*.

BELIEVE AND BE HEALED

One of the well-documented healing stories concerning Medjugorje reveals the importance of belief. Four days after his birth in 1978, Daniel Setka came down with septicaemia. He convulsed, turned blue and became rigid. He was rushed to a hospital in Mostar and remained there for a month without improvement. Additional treatments for another month at a hospital in West Germany were of no avail.

The boy's parents prayed for intercessory help and made pilgrimages to St John of Jace in Bosnia and to St Radko. Two years and nine months went by; still the child suffered and had no improvements.

In June 1981, news broke of the apparitions of Mary on Mount Podbrdo in Medjugorge. The Setkas took Daniel and their entire family to the hillside and asked the young visionaries to petition Mary for help. The visionaries, already overwhelmed with petition requests, told them to come back the next day, 29 June, the sixth day of the apparitions. After Mary appeared, one of the visionaries told the family that she had given a message for them that 'Daniel's parents were to believe firmly and the boy would be healed.'

On the way home, Daniel began showing signs of improvement. He had been unable to talk and was so frail that he could barely walk more than two steps. Now he began speaking and moving with more control. After getting home, he was soon able to stand up and walk on his own, and then run and play like any child.

No claims have been made that the healing is a 'miracle'; the family leaves that official distinction to the Church. But in the eyes of many, a miracle healing did occur. Perhaps Mary's message prompted the parents to call up their faith from the depths of their being in a way they had not done so before.

WHEN MIRACLES DO NOT HAPPEN

If belief can bring miracles, does this mean that miracles can be summoned? If so, then how do we explain cases in which a miracle is intensely desired, sought and expected – such as for a healing – and none occurs?

The answer in Christianity is that miracles are at God's discretion. This is not an entirely satisfactory answer, for it can leave a petitioner feeling unworthy or punished if a healing fails to happen. Not everyone who goes to Lourdes or other pilgrimage sites meets with desired success.

We may not fully understand all of the factors involved. For example, we may still have a barrier within us to attunement with God. We may need to do something else, either in inner work or in the external world, to achieve what we seek. And when we hold the faith for a miracle for another, we cannot know everything going on within them. Ultimately, everything, even suffering, can be seen as part of God's plan, though at times the reasons are not clear to us. But every situation, no matter how bleak, offers us the opportunity to manifest godly virtues of love, forgiveness, trust, charity, patience and so forth. We may not know how and when miracles will occur; the belief and faith in them must be held.

Co-created Miracles

What we can see now is that miracles are not entirely up to God, nor are they created entirely 'on demand' by us. Miracles are co-created. The precise recipe is beyond our understanding, and undoubtedly is different for every single case. In the perfection of all created things, miracles are possible. Sometimes we may simply need to be in the right place at the right time. Other times, our state of consciousness, our faith, our thoughts and beliefs may be pivotal in the occurrence of a miracle. Sometimes a miracle may occur in order to rekindle faith or turn a misdirected life around. Miracles are not contingent upon 'worthiness'.

We, through our hearts, minds and souls, are part of the process – not just passive receivers, but active players in the unfoldment of creation.

Let's look now at the power of prayer, which is similar to the power of thought and belief.

CHAPTER EIGHT

PRAYER AND MIRACLES

 One rainy night as he drove home from work, Tod was struck head-on by another vehicle. He was thrown from the car. When the rescue workers arrived at the scene, they were amazed to find him alive.

T he entire front end of his car was crumpled so badly that the car was nearly half its original size. Tod's injuries were so severe that his wife, Rachel, was told, 'It will be a miracle if he survives.'

Rachel sat in the hospital chapel and prayed intensely during the first critical hours. She pleaded with God to help Tod, and visualized him wrapped in a warm, loving light. She saw him healed and happy, and engaging in activities with her and the children.

Unexpectedly, Tod's condition stabilized. Not only did he recover, but he suffered very few complications from his injuries. His physicians were amazed.

Tod's survival was indeed a miracle, and Rachel gave credit to prayer, which God answered with divine healing. 'I always thought of miracles as being spectacular displays,' Rachel said. 'This accident and Tod's recovery made me realize that miracles happen all the time, and can happen to anyone.'

I have written several books on prayer and conducted

workshops on understanding prayer and making it more effective in life. I have heard countless testimonies of miracles, credited to prayer, in almost every kind of situation imaginable. One of my books, *Prayer Works*, was based on testimonials from Silent Unity, the prayer service founded by Charles and Myrtle Fillmore. Like other prayer services, Silent Unity aids millions of people every year who call or write with requests for prayer help with their problems and crises.

In my research for that book alone, I sifted through slightly more than a thousand testimonials, all sent to Unity voluntarily by people excited to share their joy. One day as I sat in the Unity library, deeply moved by the testimonials, I thought that only the most hard-headed sceptic could read these heartfelt stories and doubt the awesome power of prayer. For example:

From the depths of a thankful and joyous heart I want to give this testimony for the power of united prayer.

My young granddaughter was injured critically in a car accident. After five hours of surgery, the doctors gave her no chance for recovery, as they later informed her parents.

When we received the message of her injury at about noon that day, a very dear friend immediately called Silent Unity for your help in faith and prayer. At four o'clock that afternoon, two doctors rushed into the room where the anxious family waited and announced, 'We have just had a miracle!'

There is no way to express in words the thankfulness and the abiding faith that prayers do have an awesome power for instant healing. Our loved one is now almost recovered from a ruptured liver and crushed chest. Indeed, she expects to return to school soon.

Recently we called you asking for prayer for our nephew who was dying of leukaemia. He was bleeding to death and the doctors were unable to stop the bleeding. The hospital was running out of his type of blood.

After you prayed with me I was confident that he would improve, and the very next morning the bleeding stopped. His doctor called it a miracle. Specialists that came in from out of town to check him over just couldn't believe his healing.

Yesterday we received a report of his latest bone marrow test. The doctors thought they surely had made a mistake, for it showed complete remission. They are doing another test as they just can't believe it. We do; we expected just such results.

Healing is the most frequent prayer request. The sudden disappearance of a life-threatening illness or the instant recovery from serious injury are miracles that astonish us most. But people also experience miracles in relationships, jobs, financial fortunes, self-esteem, protection against storms and floods – and even for things that have gone missing – after they pray.

LOST AND FOUND

Carol Warner, whom we met in Chapter 1, experienced a prayer-related miracle in the return of missing personal belongings.

Carol's church sponsored popular inspirational speaker Marianne Williamson to appear at a benefit in Washington, DC. Carol volunteered to help as Williamson's driver. The night of the benefit was a rainy Friday, and during the congestion of rush hour, Carol and her minister drove to the hotel where Williamson was staying to pick her up. Carol let her minister get out of the car while she searched for a parking place. At last she managed to secure one in front of the hotel.

When Williamson and her assistant emerged from the lobby, Carol got out to open the boot of her car. She tossed her handbag – a brand new, black leather shoulder bag – onto the front seat, and left the car door open while she went around to the back to assist with the luggage. They all got in, and Carol drove to the hall where the benefit was to take place.

Carol dropped off the guests and drove away. She reached for her handbag – and got a shock when it was not there. After she parked, she searched all over the car. The bag was simply gone, along with her purse, house keys, credit cards and cosmetics kit. The purse contained about 80 dollars in cash. Carol realized that in the few seconds the handbag was unguarded on the front seat of the car, someone must have come along and snatched it.

She returned to the hotel, but of course, no one had turned in the handbag. She resigned herself to the fact that it was gone for good. She cancelled her credit cards, and the following Monday got a replacement driving licence. She spent about 120 dollars replacing her house security key and the cosmetics in her kit.

A week later, Carol was at work when a delivery man

arrived and gave her an express overnight mail package. It required her signature for receipt. The package had her office address as both the 'to' and 'from' addresses.

Carol was puzzled. She knew she hadn't ordered anything, and she certainly hadn't spent 20 dollars in postage to send herself a package.

When she opened it, she was stunned. There was her missing handbag. All of its contents were intact, including all of her credit cards and all the money in her purse. Not a dollar was missing.

There was no note of explanation. The postmark showed that the package had been sent from a low-income part of Washington, DC, quite distant from the hotel where the handbag had been taken. Whoever had returned it hadn't even taken money for the postage. The unknown sender had chosen to return the handbag to her business address – her business cards had been in her purse – rather than her home address which was on her driving licence.

Carol was elated and shared the turn of events with her mother. It seemed like a miracle not only to get the handbag back, but to get back everything in it as well. Her mother took this as news she fully expected. 'I prayed for the speedy return of your handbag with all of the contents intact,' she revealed.

And so it was.

The miracle of the returned handbag served as a reminder to Carol that anything is possible through prayer.

THE POWER OF PRAYER

Prayer is an enormous source of power and sustenance. Through prayer, we are inspired to make great triumphs, accomplishments and miraculous healings. Essentially, prayer is an act of communing with God. It makes us one with God. The 14th-century mystic, Julian of Norwich, called prayer 'one-ing with God'. Prayer is the essential link that helps us bridge two worlds, our everyday world and a transcendent reality. In that transcendent world, we see all things as being possible. And we are guided accordingly, to manifest our highest good.

The simplest and most common form of prayer is the petition, in which we ask for something for ourselves. The word 'prayer' itself means to petition, coming from the Latin term *precarius*, which means 'obtained by begging'. Most of us make petitionary prayers on an almost daily basis, informally, whenever we want something to go right in life, or when we want something to change.

Another common form of prayer is intercession. This is the prayer made to saints, holy persons and angels. We desire them to bring God's power to our benefit.

Studies of Prayer

In Chapter 6, I mentioned that the healer Olga Worrall had prayed over rye grass seedlings at a distance and stimulated them to a faster growth rate. Worrall participated in a number of scientific studies on the effects of prayer. Many other studies have been done, not only on plants but on people as well.

For example, the experiments of Reverend Franklin Loehr, a chemical engineer in Los Angeles, found that grain seeds that received positive prayer germinated and grew faster than grain seeds that received no prayer or negative prayer to inhibit their growth. The Spindrift experiments conducted by the Bruce Klingbeil family, American Christian Scientists, also showed that prayer obtained better results.

A famous prayer experiment took place at San Francisco General Hospital with patients who had suffered a heart attack. The study was 'double blind', that is, none of the doctors and health-care workers knew which patients were receiving prayer and which were not. Prayer was directed at some of the patients by persons of different religions. The prayed-for patients had less need for antibiotics, were less likely to develop complications, recovered faster, had fewer subsequent heart attacks and a lower mortality rate than the patients who received no prayer.

Japanese researchers have shown that prayer increases T-cells which fight invading viruses and bacteria. And English healer Matthew Manning has been able to significantly inhibit the growth of cancer cells through prayer, both when holding flasks containing cells and also at a distance.

Directed or Non-directed?

Is prayer more effective when it is directed to a specific desire or goal, or when non-directed, such as for the 'highest good'? Opinions are divided. People who favour directed prayer say that a specific request marshals more focused energy, and anything less is asking for potluck. People who favour non-directed prayer say that we cannot know, from our limited perspective, the outcome that is in the best interests of all concerned. If we pray for something specific, we limit our options, so we should pray for the general highest good and leave the working out of it to God.

I believe both types of prayer are effective. Studies of both directed and non-directed prayer show that both obtain results. The answer is to use both. The saints certainly did. They prayed for God's will, but they also prayed – and quite intensely – for specific things to happen.

Your heart and intuition will tell you which type of prayer is best in any given situation. Follow your own guidance.

Living Prayer

Prayer is not something we do for a few minutes a day that is separate from the rest of our activities. Every thought, word and deed is a prayer. This is the true meaning of the instruction to 'pray without ceasing' which St Paul gives in his first letter to the Thessalonians (5:17). We should consider everything we do a living prayer to God.

Healer Ambrose Worrall, husband of Olga Worrall, said we especially should be mindful of our thoughts as prayers:

Whether or not we go to church regularly, we still lead prayerful lives, though we may not know it. If we wish a man sick – it is a prayer, but a prayer for sickness, not good. If we think ill of him – it is a prayer, again of evil. If, in our mind, we see him in failure – it is a prayer for his failure. If we see him healthy, successful, if we think of him in terms of love, if we surround him and his family in our thoughts with love – this is prayer. Whatever we think about others, about ourselves, our world, becomes a prayer for or against others, for or against ourselves, for or against our world.

Becoming mindful that your thoughts and your entire life are a continuing prayer will change you in profound ways. You will develop consciousness more like the saints.

The Effect of Prayer on Miracles

Does prayer 'cause' miracles to happen? The power of prayer acts as a catalyst: it stimulates change but remains itself unchanged. Prayer opens a gateway to forces in the universe. Depending upon your point of view, these are personal attentions given by God, or the organizing forces that bind together everything in the cosmos. Prayer also helps to open up power within us,

such as our innate healing ability, and our way of knowing instantly what to do in a crisis.

Prayer activates co-creation of miracles. Change
happens within our consciousness. God answers back.

In the following story, an accident and life-threatening crisis led to an unfoldment of miracles in a partnership between a man and God.

Miracle on the Rocks

Guy R. was looking for something different in life so he
went to the Findhorn community in Scotland to stay for
a three-month programme. He took a job working in the
community kitchen. During his stay, he decided to participate in a retreat on Iona, located off the west coast of
Scotland in the Irish Sea. He had never been there, and
the wild, rocky island was reputed to be home to magic
and mystery. Guy and others who were attending the
retreat took the ferry from Mull to the island, where they
would spend the day and then return by ferry.

Iona lived up to its billing, and Guy was inspired by the terrain and primal energy. He wanted to feel connected to the land in a dramatic way. He was bored at the retreat, and so went out by himself to climb some remote steep cliffs by the sea. He had no ropes or equipment and told no one about his plans. It never occurred to him that anything disastrous would happen.

Invigorated by the sun and salty air, Guy easily clambered up a nearly vertical slope. But coming down proved to be treacherous. With a pang of unease, he wasn't certain that he would be able to navigate the rocks safely. Slowly he inched his way down, feeling for security, straining his muscles.

He was 40 to 50 feet above the beach when he had to lean out over the cliff to look for a place to put his right foot. He placed his right hand on a rocky shelf and his left hand on a large jug-hold of rock. All of sudden the jug-hold gave way.

Guy tumbled down the sharp rocks, falling about 15

or 20 feet to land on a large boulder. Intense pain shot through him, and he somehow knew his back had broken. He lay on his stomach stunned, unable to move. He wondered if he had internal injuries as well. He knew from first-aid training that he should not move, at risk of worsening the injury or even fatally snapping his spinal cord. But at least he was alive, and that was a miracle. If he just remained calm and as still as possible, someone was sure to pass by and see him, and he would be rescued.

Time passed. A lot of time. Whenever he thought a half hour had gone by, he let out cries for help. No one answered. Guy could not feel his legs. At last he summoned up the courage to twist his neck and look around. He was shocked to see that his left leg was bent at the knee and the bottom portion of the leg was pointing straight into the sky.

Then another realization hit: eventually the tide would come in and cover the place where he lay. If he were not rescued, somehow he would have to get to higher ground, or he would drown.

For a fleeting moment he thought, 'Do I lie here and die, or do I hurl myself back off this boulder and down to the ground, so I'm over it quicker?' He dismissed the dark alternatives as soon as they arose. He could not accept giving up. Surely he would be missed by the others at the retreat, and they would come looking for him. But the hours went by, and Guy still could not move, and no one came by to find him. A strange feeling of peace and calm descended over him, even as the sea edged closer.

Finally, Guy knew he had no choice but to act on his own to try to escape the tide. No matter what the consequences, he had to risk moving. He began to crawl on his belly along the rocks, away from the water. The effort was sheer horror: incredible pain, and no sensation at all of his legs.

He crawled and crawled. With each pained move, he wondered if it would be the one that might sever his spinal cord. Whenever that thought arose, he pushed it back, saying to himself, 'No, that's not going to happen.' He strove to keep positive thoughts in his mind about being rescued. Gradually, a slight tingling feeling came back in his legs.

Guy was able to crawl to the back of the bay. He looked around to try to find a way out of it. The only way was up – and he would still have to rise in order to avoid the tide. He looked around for the easiest place to start, and then began crawling up a grassy slope. The grass masked the true steepness of the incline, and Guy made slow progress. Then the grass gave way to rocks. And then another miracle happened: he discovered he had crawled to a natural ledge. It was a little shelf about four to five feet long and a foot wide. He heaved himself onto it.

From that vantage point, Guy could see that climbing further up would be impossible. Nor was there any way to go to the right or to the left. For better or worse, he would have to stay there. The sky was growing dark, and the wind was getting chillier. It began to rain on and off. Guy turned his thoughts to how he would stay warm in the cold, damp and dark. He was extremely thirsty, and knew he was seriously dehydrated.

Meanwhile, the last ferry of the day departed Iona for Mull. No one at the retreat had any inkling that Guy was in trouble. They assumed that he'd either gone back to Mull earlier, or had decided to spend the night on the island.

As he lay on the ledge, exhaustion set in. He struggled to stay awake. He was afraid that if he fell asleep he would either die of hypothermia, or he would roll off the ledge and fall to his death. So he played mind games. He counted backwards from large numbers. He savoured all the qualities of those numbers, and whether he knew someone who lived in a house with such and such a number. He sang songs and repeated mantras, especially the Aum, which he repeated over and over again like a prayer. He didn't say it as 'ohmmmm', but in its three syllables of Au-uu-mmm. It seemed to Guy that the Aum kept his internal body warmer that it might otherwise have been.

He prayed to God in the form of intentions: 'I will survive and I will live, and I will live well.' He thought about the process of living after this ordeal was over, and that it might be hard for him, but he was determined to make it. He also continued his periodic cries for help, but his voice grew weaker and weaker. Somehow he made it through the night.

At dawn the next morning he could see fishing boats passing by not far offshore. He waved frantically to them and shouted, but no one noticed him. Boats continued to pass by throughout the day, but he could not get the attention of anyone on board them. He was a mere dot on the rocks, lost in the landscape. A sailing boat came close to shore, about 50 yards from the mouth of the bay. Guy yelled at the man aboard and waved, but the man did not see or hear him. In despair, Guy cursed the man, but as the boat sailed past, he shouted, 'I love you, anyway! I forgive you!'

It became apparent to Guy that he wasn't going to be spotted and rescued. He began to crawl back down the cliff that he so painfully had crawled up. He thought perhaps he had made a mistake and there really was another way out. There *was* no other way, but he didn't know that. He was descending to a certain death, for he would not have the energy to return to the ledge.

While Guy was crawling down, another miracle happened: he was discovered by a man who happened to be out walking on the road above the cliff. The man asked three other walkers who were in the vicinity to stay with Guy while he summoned help. They were reluctant to do so, at which point Guy's composure dissolved. Seeing his distress, they agreed.

The Coast Guard was unable to reach him, and so a helicopter was brought in to airlift Guy out. It was nightfall by the time he was admitted to a small hospital and his broken back X-rayed. It rained hard, and as the rain beat on the windows of his room, Guy could not help but think that if he were still on the ledge, he surely would have died during the second night. He had been rescued in the nick of time. What a miracle!

The next day Guy was moved to a hospital in Glasgow. He had an operation, during which his spine was reinforced with metal and a piece of his pelvic bone. Doctors warned him that he probably would never regain full flexibility in his spine, and he might not be able to walk without pain, or perhaps even walk at all.

Guy was visited by his co-workers and friends from Findhorn, who began praying for him, individually and also as a group. Every day during the community's meditation and prayer period, prayers were said for him. A strengthening spiritual energy flowed through him.

Guy's recovery was painful, but much faster than was expected. A cage-like brace was put around his spine. Determined to regain his full mobility, he took hesitant steps and managed to climb up and down a few stairs.

The day he took his first trip outside the hospital was sunny and beautiful. He staggered outside and found a tree. He lay down under it and put his hands up to the trunk. He felt wonderfully connected to the soul of the tree, and to all Nature. 'Thank you,' he said to God. And from then on, every time he walked, he said, 'Thank you, thank you for these steps.'

Guy left the hospital and went to Lincoln to recuperate at his brother's home. He forced himself to walk, even though a small effort was excruciatingly painful, and would leave him exhausted for hours. Twenty-eight days after his fall, he danced in a circle dance, and spent the following day in bed from the pain. But soon he went out with a mountaineering club and did a ten-mile walk in the Black Mountains of Wales, managing to climb to the top of a peak. The following year, he was back at

Findhorn, walking without brace or difficulty, and dancing in the seasonal festivities. His recovery was nothing short of a miracle.

'I know there's a reason for my experience, and a reason why I lived,' Guy said. 'It's definitely strengthened my belief in God. I know I can call on that power whenever I need it. Nothing is impossible.'

Guy's experience was not just one miracle, but an unfolding series of miracles. It was extraordinary that he survived the fall and was able to crawl to a ledge that afforded him safety. Had he crawled a foot or two to either side, he might have missed the ledge altogether. Once there, the darkest and most difficult part of his ordeal took place: he had to combat the elements, exhaustion, shock and dehydration just to stay alive. He accomplished this miracle by prayer.

Guy did not beg God in prayer to save him. Rather, he prayed his intention to live, and this gave him strength to persevere and do what seemed impossible. He stayed awake during that terrible night; he was rescued; he regained his ability to walk and his flexibility to climb and dance.

The Aum mantra was also a powerful prayer for Guy. In Eastern thought, Aum is the most sacred and comprehensive expression of spiritual knowledge. It is a symbol of form and a manifestation of spiritual power. It represents supreme consciousness, reality and truth. The vibration of Aum brings the soul into contact with the Absolute. For Guy, it was a prayer that formed a lifeline to God, the greatest power in the universe, the power from which miracles flow.

We are not the passive recipients of miracles. We actively participate in the creation of them, whether we are aware of it or not. Our intentionality – our thoughts, beliefs, faith, intent, will, prayer and expectation – influence their manifestation. The miracles may happen to us personally, or may happen on a broader scale

– perhaps even far away from us, at a distant point on the planet.

What can we do to develop our 'miracle consciousness'?

CHAPTER NINE

CONSCIOUS MIRACLES

    Our active role in the co-creation of miracles in no way detracts or subtracts from God. God, the centre of creation, is the source of all being from which all else emanates.

From God flows a power that manifests in miracles. Through our consciousness, we interact with that power.

Perhaps the grand public displays of miracles described in the Bible were necessary because group consciousness expected God to intervene dramatically in the affairs of humanity. The group consciousness was disempowered; only certain holy people chosen by God were empowered.

This disempowerment may have been necessary to prevent miraculous abilities from being used improperly. God's intent, however, is for all of us to realize our full capabilities – Jesus reminded people that they would do his works and greater – so it is certainly part of our growth and evolution to become increasingly empowered and able to bring about the miraculous. But we can only do so if we also grow in stature spiritually. Such abilities must not be used for selfish purpose but to aid and benefit life.

The research into psi, field consciousness, thought and prayer shows that there are currents of energy running in the background of all things at all times. The current of miracles is like this. The currents are fed and accessed by thought, belief, faith, prayer, affirmation, will, expectation, words and actions. The more we develop our spiritual side through love, virtues and devotion, the higher we raise all of those other factors. They become part of our *intention*.

INTENTIONALITY

Our intention is a combination of our determination, objective, aim and desire. 'Intentionality' is gaining more attention in scientific studies of why prayer works, and why some people seem to 'think' themselves well.

Intentionality is both conscious and subconscious. Our subconscious thoughts have an effect on manifestation just as do our conscious thoughts. Before we can have clarity of intention, both need to be brought into alignment. 'Perhaps our greatest personal challenge is learning to discern the origin and intent of our conscious and subconscious motives,' says Ann Nunley, co-president of the International Society for the Study of Subtle Energy Medicine, based in Boulder, Colorado. 'If we wish to exercise our intentions by means of conscious motives, we must be willing to look within and do the personal clearing that will allow us to move towards authentic integrity.'

Many miracles do not seem to be the result of conscious intent. When miraculous rescue has occurred in emergencies, only the intervening hand of God seems evident to many people. One doesn't have time to think or consciously set an intention – only to react instinctively.

If we look closely at such cases, however, we do find elements of subconscious intention. In the flash of the moment, instant prayers are made (even 'I don't want to die!' is a prayer), or there is an elevated state of consciousness that is instantly able to influence forces in motion. Perhaps other influencing factors in a miracle can be found in the experiencer's overall consciousness shaped by habits of prayer, meditation, connectedness and so on – as well as by group consciousness. We have layers and layers of intention permeating our consciousness.

Thus, synchronicities – 'meaningful coincidences' – and events that happen seemingly 'out of the blue' are not happenstance at all, but an ordering of circumstances as the result of consciousness.

No certain miracle-making formula exists, at least known to us at present. However, we can make changes in our daily lives that profoundly affect our consciousness and stimulate and strengthen the divine currents around us. Thus, we can become more open to the possibility of miracles, both those that affect us directly and personally, and those that create circumstances beneficial to humanity as a whole. We *can* change the world, and the process starts with the individual. In the words of Robert H. Coxon, 'You have to create miracles on the inside first. When you have faith and know you can do it, then all you have to do is ask.'

Here is a plan for creating 'conscious miracles':

Step 1: Find a Spiritual Home

Your sense of connection to everything is greatly enhanced when you have a spiritual path: a religious or mystical tradition, a philosophy, a point of view about creation. Go where your heart leads you. Miracles are democratic.

Devote time to study of spiritual, philosophical and metaphysical ideas to expand your world view. Be open to a broad spectrum of possibilities. The narrower your focus, the narrower your consciousness.

Allow the power of God to manifest in ways that are meaningful to you. This may involve intercessory figures such as saints, Mary, angels or protective loved ones on the Other Side. Or, it may involve a more abstract relationship with Universal Mind.

Step 2: Establish your Intention

As Kryon teaches, 'there is no greater power in the universe than human intent and love', which are the main catalysts for miracles.

What is it you wish to manifest in life? There is no such thing as irrevocable 'fate'. We may come into life with an overall purpose or life plan in our soul, but we have myriad ways of working it out.

Manifestation occurs on various levels – ordinary things in ordinary life, or things pertaining to higher consciousness. There's nothing wrong with pursuing goals in the material world – career, health, financial security and so forth – but the loftier your goals, the more you become a miracle-worker. The saints sought only to love God and do his will.

In addition to your personal goals, set higher ones, such as being an instrument of peace and love, or helping to improve the lives of others.

Step 3: Be Open to Possibilities

Narrow-mindedness and limited vision shut off miracle consciousness. Be open to how your goals work out, and be open to new directions. Life is a process of unfoldment.

Step 4: Spend Time Every Day in Prayer or Meditation

Prayer and meditation are two of the best and quickest ways to elevate consciousness and make space for divine light to come into the soul. Subtle, then profound, shifts of awareness occur. Prayer and meditation strengthen faith, which Hebrews 11:1 tells us is 'the assurance of things hoped for, the conviction of things not seen'.

Step 5: Take Responsibility

Take responsibility not only for your own life, but for your influence on the whole. The whole of humanity and the whole of creation are as good as the individuals in them. Negativity hurts not just yourself, but degrades group consciousness.

Step 6: Practise Virtues

Be mindful of bringing virtues into your thoughts, speech and actions: love, charity, forgiveness, humility, patience, faith, and so on. Practising virtues elevates consciousness – besides helping others.

Step 7: Practise Good Thinking

Every day we entertain a flood of thoughts and emotions ranging from love to hate, ecstasy to anger or sadness. It would be superhuman to police them all – but a mind-fulness about them brings about substantial improve-ment. Let negative thoughts go and replace them with positive ones. We manifest what we think about. Use positive thoughts and affirmations. Let go of doubt and fear.

Improved thought leads to improved words and action. Think before speaking negatively and before acting. Make immediate amends when things do go wrong.

Step 8: Love Yourself as well as God

Loving yourself sounds narcissistic to many ears, but understood correctly it is one of the fundamentals of spiritual Truth. By loving yourself, you appreciate yourself as a wonderful creation of God. Loving yourself allows the power of God to unfold through you. You cannot truly help others until you love yourself. Otherwise, you operate from a standpoint of deficiency and neediness.

The glue that binds everything together in this universe is love.

Step 9: Learn to Let Go

If you are full of old baggage, how can there be room for anything new? Many of us are filled to the brim with old emotional stuff that does not serve us well. Release old business, old wounds, self-doubts, fears and attachments. Forgive old hurts.

Doing an inner tune-up may require a lot of work on your part. You may even need outside help, such as counselling. It may take time. But once you start the process, spiritual benefits come immediately.

Forgiveness brought an immediate miracle of healing to Dr Joan Pizzino. She had gone to Grand Cayman Island in the Bahamas for a scuba-diving holiday with her fiancé, Lee. A terrible incident occurred, in which they were attacked. A man armed with a club and knife engaged Lee in combat and attempted to kill him. The reason for the attack never became known. But the attacker was arrested, tried, convicted and jailed.

Joan and Lee married, but Joan was overwhelmed by long-lasting physical and psychological trauma. The marriage did not survive.

For 13 years, Joan suffered intermittent neck pain, which she ascribed to poor sleeping positions or general discomfort. Then suddenly the pain escalated in severity, and her entire body became affected. It felt as though a knife or an axe were stuck in her neck. She lost muscle strength and dropped objects. She could no longer sit up, so she either stood or lay on the floor. Eventually, even lying on the floor was too painful, and for three days she stood up to sleep. She tried different therapies with no success.

Finally, she had an MRI (magnetic resonance imaging) scan, which revealed bone spurs pressing upon her spinal cord. She was told she had myelopathy and was urged to have immediate surgery to avoid becoming a quadriplegic. The idea of surgery was frightening. As a doctor, Joan also knew that spinal surgery does not always bring relief. Nonetheless, she scheduled the operation – only to cancel it nine hours before she was to go under the knife.

At the recommendation of a friend, Joan began energy healing treatments that included Reiki and the Barbara Brennan system. She tapped into past life memories of having an axe buried in her back and a knife in her neck. One day, as she lay on the floor listening to a self-help tape by Carolyn Myss about healing and forgiveness, it flashed on Joan that she had never forgiven the attacker on Cayman Island. What happened next was this:

Although I had previously wished him dreadful tortures in prison, I was more than willing to forgive him, and, in fact, thanked him for setting in motion all the events of

*my marriage and divorce that had led me to where I was
that day.* In that instant, my pain disappeared and I
was able to sit up and do all the things I wanted to
do. *Although I had never been a particularly religious
person, during the healing service at the end of the tape,
I was overtaken by a joy more profound than any I had
ever known. I felt that knives would no longer be a part
of my life. I believed that the bone spurs had been
'zapped'. While that may or may not be true, I now
unshakeably* know *that God exists.*

Joan had made the discovery that healing really is being
whole. Resentments, grudges, wounds and anger prevent
us from becoming whole. Love and forgiveness restore us
to wholeness. No wrong exists that cannot be restored to
wholeness.

Step 10: Keep Joy at Centre-stage

People whose lives abound in miracles and good fortune have a high measure of joy. That doesn't mean they go about in a state of bliss all the time, but that life is essentially joyful to them, regardless of its ups and downs.

In my book *The Miracle of Prayer: True Stories of Blessed Healings*, I cited a 12-week study of 'ordinary people' who undertook a daily prayer for the 'fruit of the spirit' found in Galatians 5:22–3: 'But the fruit of the Spirit is love, joy, peace, patience, kindness, goodness, faithfulness, gentleness, self-control: against such there is no law.' The participants prayed an average of six days a week, preferably in the morning. Some prayed for a few minutes, others for longer periods.

Almost all the participants were surprised at how quickly they felt significant inner shifts and changes. They especially felt filled with love and joy. These inner changes in turn created changes in their outer environment. They made deeper connections to others, appreciated more things, felt less stressed and dealt with problems differently.

Your outer world reflects your inner world. Inner chaos and tumult create a stress-filled world. Inner love and joy create a peaceful world – one in which miracles are more likely to happen.

Step 11: Practise Presence

Presence is being 'in the flow' of 'everything that is'. Presence is living in the moment, appreciating it and being open to possibilities. We are present when we are not mulling over what is past or fixated on what 'needs' to happen in the future.

In his book *Everyday Miracles*, David Spangler, an American visionary who was a key figure in the early days of Findhorn, says the energy of presence 'widens and opens the latticed mesh of our reality not by opposing or challenging it but by becoming part of it, blending with it, and through its own expandedness, expanding the mesh as a whole. Then there is space, there is openness, there is a potential for something new to emerge, for reality to shift, and for miracles to happen.'

Spangler says that he often feels an uplift or a heightened sense of energy when a 'manifestation moment' occurs. I have experienced the same. In my book on soulmates, I tell one of the more dramatic moments, which came when I was walking on a beach in Oregon at sunset time. It was the night of the full moon. As the sun was sinking into the sea, the moon was rising over the coastal range mountains. I was admiring the beauty of it when suddenly I felt an incredible uplift. The forces of the universe – represented by the opposites of sun and moon, earth and sky, day and night, masculine and feminine – seemed poised in perfect balance. I was outside of time. I 'knew' all this intuitively without having to think about it. I also 'knew' and 'saw' that cosmic

forces in motion could go any number of ways in rela-
tion to my life, and however I set my intention, it would
come to pass. I 'knew' that setting my intention in this
timelessness would have more power. I quickly made
three wishes. And as soon as the moment was upon me,
it was gone, and reality seemed 'ordinary' again.

The wishes all came true. Yes, they might have come
true, anyway. But the power and sense of connectedness
to all things, which happened in an instant, has stayed
with me for years. I was able to experience this moment
simply by being present. I was not caught up in an inner
monologue or preoccupied with concerns.

Dr Joan Pizzino calls her healing through forgiveness
a 'Holy Instant'. The miracle, she said, 'occurred in the
infinitesimal instant in which I made a choice to forgive'. The experience made Joan realize how everything
is inextricably linked: past and present, life and life, person and person.

I have contacted the joy of the Divine many times since then as I actively work to live in the moment-to-moment reality of All That Is. I now believe we are spiritual beings having a human experience, and that probably all illness is merely one of the few ways that the Spirit has to get in touch with us. I never did find out why [the man on Cayman] tried to kill us that day in 'paradise' but I now believe it was part of my Soul's Purpose to bring this miracle to me. It is now my profoundest desire to facilitate this process for others who suffer, and to 'hold the space': that will allow them to be touched by God, as I was.

The 'Holy Instant' moments, as Joan calls them, are not capricious but come as the result of conscious choice. Being present is a choice that enables us to recognize and act on the moments when they do occur. Most of us keep our minds so busy that we are not present – we are living consciously either in the past or the unmanifest future. These special moments arise, and we miss them entirely.

Presence arises from following the above points. A spiritual path, prayer and meditation, study, practice of virtues and right thinking impregnate consciousness at a deep level. They become forces at work below the surface of the mind, acting to place us in the right circumstances for something miraculous to manifest. Presence allows miracles to unfold. Practising presence increases the opportunities for 'manifestation moments'.

We have the ability to create in partnership with the divine an exciting world of peace and enhanced well-being and happiness. Miracles are both a gift from God and a gift of innate ability. When we fully awaken to this truth and accept it, the miraculous will unfold in ways we can only now imagine. We can bring what we imagine into being.

AN ANGEL IN YOUR POCKET

Rosemary Ellen Guiley

They don't wear wings, they don't live on clouds, but they *do* come into our lives ... Throughout history artists have painted them, poets have written about them, and films have portrayed them. But angels are more than figments of our imagination – they are real and have changed the lives of many ordinary people.

Bestselling author and teacher Rosemary Ellen Guiley answers questions including: who are they? what are they? where do they come from? This is an angel guide you can carry around in your pocket – making sure your guardian angel is always with you!

ISBN 0 7225 3967 3